Displaying
Your Findings

Sixth Edition

Displaying Your Findings

A Practical Guide for Creating Figures, Posters, and Presentations

Adelheid A. M. Nicol and Penny M. Pexman

American Psychological Association • *Washington, DC*

Published by
American Psychological Association
750 First Street, NE
Washington, DC 20002
www.apa.org

To order
APA Order Department
P.O. Box 92984
Washington, DC 20090-2984
Tel: (800) 374-2721; Direct: (202) 336-5510
Fax: (202) 336-5502; TDD/TTY: (202) 336-6123
Online: www.apa.org/books/
E-mail: order@apa.org

In the U.K., Europe, Africa, and the Middle East, copies may be ordered from
American Psychological Association
3 Henrietta Street
Covent Garden, London
WC2E 8LU England

Typeset in Sabon, Futura, and Univers by Circle Graphics, Inc., Columbia, MD

Printer: United Book Press, Baltimore, MD
Cover Designer: Naylor Design, Washington, DC

The opinions and statements published are the responsibility of the authors, and such opinions and statements do not necessarily represent the policies of the American Psychological Association.

Library of Congress Cataloging-in-Publication Data

Nicol, Adelheid A. M.
  Displaying your findings : a practical guide for creating figures, posters, and presentations / Adelheid A. M. Nicol and Penny M. Pexman. — 6th ed.
      p. cm.
  Includes bibliographical references and index.
  ISBN-13: 978-1-4338-0707-7 (alk. paper)
  ISBN-10: 1-4338-0707-6 (alk. paper)
  1. Psychological literature. 2. Psychology—Graphic methods. 3. Psychology—Posters. 4. Poster presentations. I. Pexman, Penny M. II. Title.
  BF76.8.N53 2010
  001.4'226—dc22
                                        2009038684

British Library Cataloguing-in-Publication Data
A CIP record is available from the British Library.

Printed in the United States of America
Sixth Edition

Contents

Preface

Our first book, *Presenting Your Findings: A Practical Guide for Creating Tables,*[1] provided examples and specified important elements of effective tables. We wrote the book because as graduate students and then as new faculty members, we had often struggled to figure out the best way to present our findings in tables. After that book was published in 1999, several individuals contacted us, wondering whether the same type of book existed for figures. In response, we wrote the first edition of the present book, which was published in 2003, hoping once again to facilitate the process of presenting research findings.

In this revised edition, our primary purpose is to help people present their findings in an effective way. We hope that by presenting numerous examples, explanatory bubbles, and quick-reference checklists, we will save readers some time in creating their figures. Most important, we hope that readers can use elements of the sample figures and visuals in the book to enhance their own work. The success of this book will be defined by its usefulness.

Revised Edition

This revised edition of *Displaying Your Findings* was motivated by a number of developments, including the release of the sixth edition of the *Publication Manual of the American Psychological Association.*[2] Since the first edition of *Displaying Your Findings* was published, the presentation of hand-drawn figures and the use of slide projectors and overhead projectors have become almost obsolete. Most journal submissions are

---

[1]Nicol, A. A. M., & Pexman, P. M. (1999). *Presenting your findings: A practical guide for creating tables.* Washington, DC: American Psychological Association.

[2]American Psychological Association. (2010). *Publication manual of the American Psychological Association* (6th ed.). Washington, DC: Author.

conducted electronically; researchers can easily draw and subsequently print their figures for reports and theses using personal computers and printers. Some APA Style guidelines have changed (the previous edition of *Displaying Your Findings* was based on the 5th ed. of the *Publication Manual*). Furthermore, some reporting standards for statistics have changed. The following list outlines some of the changes from the previous edition of *Displaying Your Findings*:

1. Many figures include confidence intervals (this is particularly true for bar graphs and line graphs).
2. If researchers wish to use color in their figure or present numerous images in an article intended for publication, they should first check the journal submission guidelines or department and university guidelines to determine acceptability of color figures and pictures and the specifications of those color figures (e.g., image size in terms of bytes) and to determine whether the journal publishes color figures or offers alternative online-only publication venues for those particular figures. It is up to the individual researcher to determine whether color should be used in conference posters or presentations.
3. The font for each figure caption matches the rest of the text.
4. The font size in a figure can be as small as 8 points or as large as 14 points but not smaller or larger.
5. Text in the figure can be single-, one-and-a-half-, or double-spaced. Text in the figure caption should be double-spaced.
6. As before, each figure appears on its own page, but now figure captions are placed on the same page below the figure rather than on a separate page.
7. The preference is to not use a lot of different types of shading. Ideally, any shading used should make it easy to distinguish one object (e.g., bar) from another (e.g., gray, black, and white). The *Publication Manual* indicates a preference for no more than three types of shading.

Acknowledgments

In writing both versions of this book, we received assistance from many people. We thank all of the reviewers for their useful comments; our research assistants; and the staff of APA Books, who made this a pleasurable experience.

Adelheid Nicol dedicates this book to her husband, Yves Mayrand, and their three children, Ariane, Amélie, and Mathieu. Penny Pexman dedicates this book to her husband, Dave Pexman, and their two children, John and Kate.

Displaying
Your Findings

Introduction

This book assists readers in designing figures following the guidelines of the sixth edition of the *Publication Manual of the American Psychological Association* (APA).[1] It does so by providing numerous examples of figures constructed to accompany fictional studies. We describe the studies in sufficient detail to illustrate how the figures were created. In the same manner, we also illustrate the preparation of effective posters and visual aids for conference presentations. We hope that this method of describing the development of figures and conference materials will inspire researchers to be creative in producing clear, rich, and concise presentations of their results.

When to Use a Figure

Figures can be extremely helpful to a reader. They can be used to simplify complex information that would be difficult or lengthy to express in words, such as structural equation models, experiment apparatus, or results. Figures present data or findings directly and tell a story, sometimes instantaneously, whereas tables, for example, require the reader to analyze the individual components to understand the message being conveyed. Figures can summarize or emphasize certain findings, illustrate complicated results such as interaction effects, and show patterns of data. They may also be used to demonstrate a progression of results, such as trends, or to accentuate a crucial point or change in the results. The goal of using figures is to help the reader better understand the material and grasp its essential aspects.

Authors should not use any figure that does not contribute to the reader's understanding of the information or that is redundant with the text. Figures that are too

---

[1] American Psychological Association. (2010). *Publication manual of the American Psychological Association* (6th ed.). Washington, DC: Author.

complicated and require a lot of explanation should not be used. Furthermore, if a figure does not have a professional appearance, then it is best not to include it. A good figure is one that is easy to understand, presents findings in a clear manner, summarizes information, and requires little interpretation.

Anatomy of a Figure

All figures consist of both the visual image to be presented (i.e., graph, plot, drawing, chart, or photograph) and the caption. The figure caption usually includes descriptive information regarding the figure, an explanation of abbreviations and symbols presented in the figure, and a permission credit line if the figure was published elsewhere. In addition, sometimes a legend is included to help the reader interpret the image. Figure 1.1 illustrates the main components of a commonly used type of figure—the line graph.

Figure 1.1. ◄········ Note: This figure number is for the purpose of the present book only and should not be included in a manuscript.

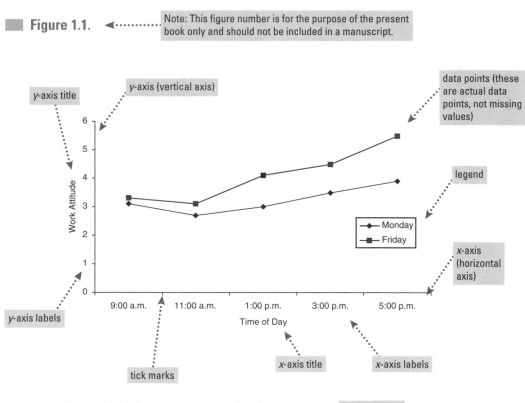

Figure X. Main components of a figure. ◄······ figure caption

Organization of the Book

There are so many types and styles of figures that it would be difficult to present them all in a single book. We have thus limited the scope of this book to examples of the types of figures more commonly found in the psychology literature.

In designing this book, we have, to a certain extent, used APA's categorization of figures: Everything that is not text, a table, or an exhibit[2] is considered to be a figure. We present 11 different kinds of figures: bar graphs, histograms, line graphs, plots, drawings, combination graphs (which combine graphs or incorporate drawings or photographs with graphs), pie graphs, dendrograms, stem-and-leaf plots, charts, and photographs. After examining the literature, we found that bar graphs, line graphs, plots, drawings, charts, and photographs were the types of figures that were most commonly found in psychology journals. These figures also tend to be easy to comprehend and summarize a large amount of information very well. Although the other types of figures mentioned are not as commonly found in the literature, we thought it was important to incorporate them in this book to present other possible examples on which researchers can model their figures because each type of figure is used to present a different kind of information.

Unlike our book on tables, the chapters in the present book are not organized according to type of analysis. Figures are not always essential, so we did not wish to mislead readers by organizing the book by statistics. Instead, we have organized the book by type of figure, and each type of figure is described in a separate chapter. In addition, the last two chapters provide guidelines for preparing poster presentations for conferences and visuals (e.g., PowerPoint slides) for presentations. Some types of figures are so rarely used that we did not include them in this book. This does not mean that authors cannot use them in a manuscript; authors simply should follow APA Style guidelines and the checklists we provide as closely as possible. Exhibit 1.1 is a description of the various parts of each chapter.

A Few Caveats

The figures presented in this book are intended to be used as models to assist researchers in designing their own figures. The example research studies on which they are based are greatly simplified; we do not claim that the example studies provide the best means of conducting a study or illustrate the best ways to analyze data. This book is not a research methods book or a statistics book, and we have not presented theoretical explanations for the example studies because our focus is data presentation, not experimental design. In most instances, descriptive and inferential statistics have not been provided because these should be presented in the text of the manuscript or within tables. For the same reason, we have not presented all of the information that should be presented when reporting results. Furthermore, some information presented in figures could instead be presented in text or in tables, depending on the preferences of the researcher. Finally, all of the examples provided are fictional. Any likeness to actual studies is purely coincidental.

---

[2]Exhibits are primarily used in books rather than journal articles; they generally do not include the basic components of a table (see section 5.08 of the 6th ed. of the *Publication Manual*). Examples of exhibits include bulleted lists, dialogue, or significant points an author would like to highlight in a particular section.

■ Exhibit 1.1.

Chapter Sections in This Book

What Type of Data Is Presented?

The first section of each chapter explains the type of data or information presented in the figure highlighted in that chapter (e.g., change in scores over time or over a number of trials) and includes a description of the figure's features, including subtypes.

Example

In the Example section, we briefly describe a fictional study. We have included examples from different areas of psychology, such as clinical psychology, cognitive psychology, developmental psychology, educational psychology, industrial/organizational psychology, neuroscience, and social psychology. If the results of a statistical procedure (e.g., multidimensional scaling) or a specific type of data (e.g., event-related potentials) are presented, then we briefly describe that procedure or data. A list of variables, presented in a box following the description of the study, includes the study variables for the example to help the reader identify the key elements of the study.

Figures

The figures constructed for the fictional study constitute the bulk of each chapter. Text bubbles accompanying each figure enclose explanatory comments. More than one version of the same figure may be presented to show acceptable variations in figure elements. Each figure is identified by a figure number denoting both the number of the chapter in this book and the order of the figure within the chapter (e.g., Figure 2.6 is the sixth figure in Chapter 2). Figures illustrating sample figures (as opposed to figures illustrating sample posters and visuals for presentations) have a second figure number and a figure caption representative of what would actually appear in a manuscript. These figure captions begin with the words *Figure X,* with the *X* representing the appropriate figure number in the hypothetical research described in the example.

Checklist of Effective Elements

We present checklists of elements that make a figure or presentation particularly useful and attention getting and that conform to APA guidelines. The checklist at the end of this first chapter is a general checklist that applies to all of the figures presented in this book. For convenience, this general checklist is also presented inside the front cover of the book. In addition, other chapters contain more specific checklists that apply to the types of figures or visual presentations discussed in those chapters.

Guidelines for Preparing Figures

The manner in which the data are presented is crucial for comprehension. The author's or presenter's primary goal always should be to ensure that the audience understands the research project. Otherwise, the impact of the research is compromised.

Most of the figures in this book were originally created using widely accessible programs such as Microsoft Word, Microsoft PowerPoint, and Microsoft Excel. Any software that the user feels comfortable with and that produces graphics with clearly distinguishable lines, shapes, shades, and contrasts is acceptable. Many journal and book publishers have very specific requirements about figure format, and authors are expected to follow them. Figures 1.2 and 1.3 illustrate how to submit a figure for publication.

Tips and Tricks for Creating Figures

Although the computer programs we used to create the figures in this book can easily produce simple graphs, if a graph or drawing differed slightly from the menu options provided by these programs, we had to use creative methods to produce the effects that we needed. For instance, Figure 4.15 (see p. 58) presents diagonal lines on the y-axis to represent a break, but these lines cannot be automatically drawn by the programs that we used. To create these lines, we had to draw three lines, two black and one white, placed side by side (the snap-to-grid feature of these programs may have to be disabled in order to do this). The three objects are then selected, grouped, and rotated using the drawing menu functions. Figure 1.4 illustrates how these lines were created (the lines were placed on a gray background here to make them easy to distinguish), and Figure 1.5 illustrates how they would look once placed on a line graph.

In Figure 1.5, the numbers 4, 7, 10, 13, 16, and 19 are changed to boldface by drawing a text box and manually typing in these values in boldface, then placing the text box directly over the x-axis values that have been automatically placed using the word processor's chart function. The boldface function cannot be used for the individual numbers under the chart menu of these programs.

To create Figure 1.6, we had to include spaces when entering the data. So, in the first row of data entry where the x-axis labels were entered, we included a blank space for every change in treatment that is shown (i.e., 1, 2, 3, 4, blank, 5, 6, 7, blank, 8, 9, 10, blank, etc.). In the second row, where the data are first entered, we also included a blank space for every change in treatment (i.e., 1-year data points: 20.4, 27.4, 30.0, 20.4, blank, 14.0, 15.0, 13.0, blank, 20.0, 21.0, 19.0, blank, etc.). Once the graph was completed, white boxes were created and placed on the x-axis where the blank spaces are supposed to occur (i.e., between numbers 4 and 5, 7 and 8, 10 and 11, 13 and 14, etc.). This is one of many possible ways to create such effects.

A few other graphs required various manipulations. We cannot describe them all because this is not the purpose of this book, and it is up to the readers to determine how creative they wish to be and how comfortable they are with drawing using the computer. In addition, it is important to note that as programs evolve, the options provided to the user in these graphing menus may also change.

General Guidelines for Figures

The following guidelines for preparing figures are relevant for any manuscript, not only those submitted to journals or edited volumes requiring APA Style. Therefore,

■ **Figure 1.2.**

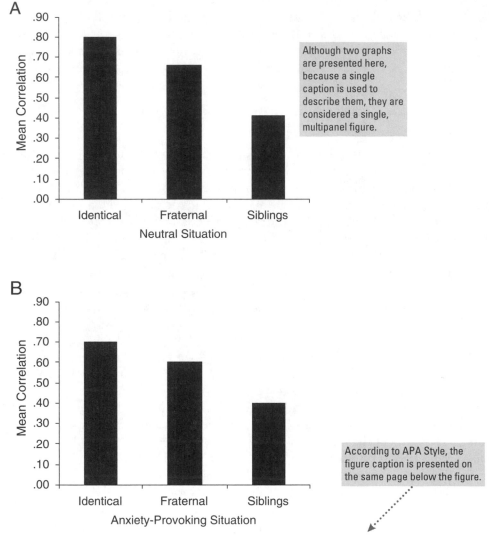

Figure X. Average correlation coefficients of identical, fraternal, and sibling dyads' emotional intelligence self-ratings in a neutral (A) and an anxiety-provoking (B) situation.

Figure 1.3.

This is Figure 2 of a sample manuscript.

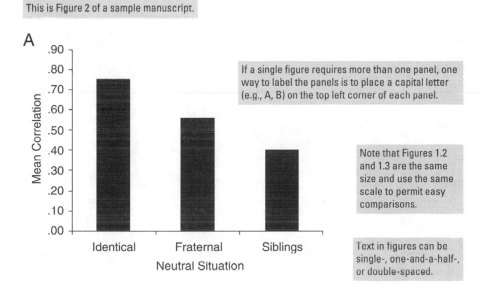

A

If a single figure requires more than one panel, one way to label the panels is to place a capital letter (e.g., A, B) on the top left corner of each panel.

Note that Figures 1.2 and 1.3 are the same size and use the same scale to permit easy comparisons.

Text in figures can be single-, one-and-a-half-, or double-spaced.

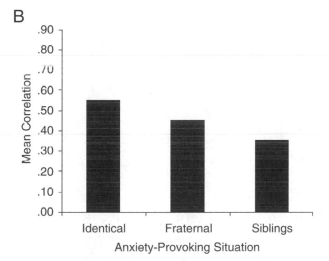

Figure X. Average correlation coefficients of identical, fraternal, and sibling dyads' scores on emotional intelligence as rated by an independent observer in a neutral (A) and an anxiety-provoking (B) situation.

Figure captions should be double-spaced in the manuscript (not shown here).

Figure 1.4. Illustration of How to Draw Double Slashes

Figure 1.5.

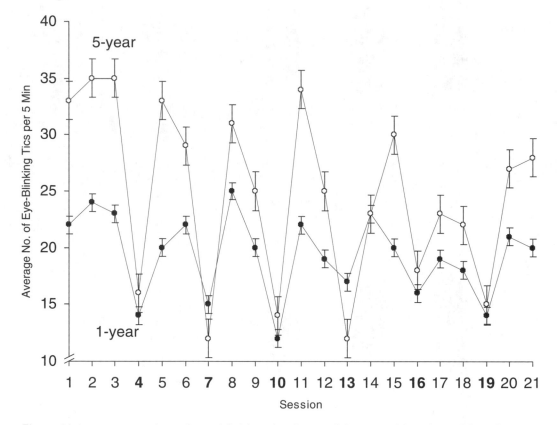

Figure X. Average number of eye-blinking tics for participants with a tic problem for up to 1 year (*n* = 17; black circles) and for participants with a tic problem for a minimum of 5 years (*n* = 15; white circles). Standard errors are also provided. The *x*-axis labels in boldface denote measures taken immediately after an aerobics class.

Figure 1.6.

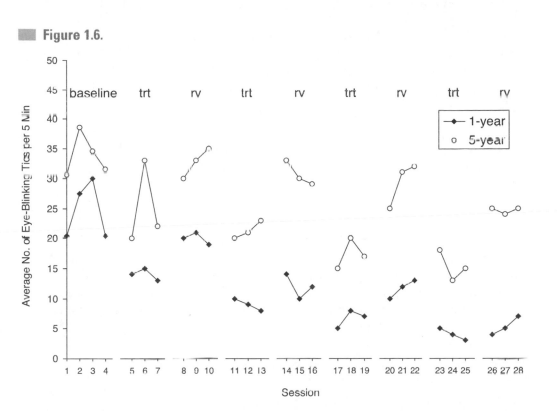

Figure X. Average number of eye-blinking tics for participants with this problem for up to 1 year (*n* = 24) and for participants with this problem for a minimum of 5 years (*n* = 18). trt = treatment; rv = reversal.

they also should be followed in preparing figures for theses, manuscripts not to be published, and manuscripts submitted to journals or edited volumes not requiring APA Style.

- The figure must be relevant to the manuscript and play a key role in the section in which it is mentioned (e.g., Introduction, Method, Results, and Discussion). Some journals permit publication of additional figures online. These figures are not essential to the manuscript but provide information that can enhance certain points made in the manuscript.

- The figure image should be as simple as possible; only essential information should be included.

- Labels should be as concise as possible.

- Carefully consider the use of color to determine whether it is necessary. Most journals and books are printed in black and white, so it is important to check with the publisher to determine whether they accept color in figures (and whether this is the same for simple figures—e.g., line art—or complex figures—e.g., brain scans). Some journals permit the submission of supplemental material[3] that will be published online but not on paper. This supplemental material could be in color even if print material is not. Theses and reports are printed in color or black and white, depending on depart-

---

[3]For more on supplemental material and online supplemental archives, see section 2.13 of the sixth edition of the *Publication Manual.* For more on the use of color in figures, see sections 5.04, 5.25, and 5.27–5.29.

ment and university guidelines. Color can be used effectively in conference posters or presentations.

■ Guidelines regarding image file size need to be verified.

■ Avoid clutter such as grids, patterns, unnecessary colors, or three-dimensional graphs.

■ The units of measurement should be specified within the figure.

■ A figure should be understandable on its own. All information needed to interpret the figure (e.g., abbreviations, definitions) should be included in the caption. Little explanation should be required in the text.

■ Multiple figures in the same manuscript should be consistent in size, labeling, text font, patterns used, and legend style.

■ The figure should be presented as close as possible to where it is mentioned in the text. This can be easily accomplished for reports and theses if the figures are not required to be presented all together at the end of the paper; departmental and university guidelines on this point need to be verified beforehand. For manuscripts to be submitted for publication, journal guidelines will dictate where they are to be placed. Further, even though the author may indicate where the figure should be placed, the typesetter may not be able to place the figure precisely where the author wishes.

■ Authors need to verify departmental, university, or publisher guidelines regarding the file type in which the figure is to be saved and its resolution.

Guidelines for Figures That Follow APA Style

In addition to the general guidelines, several other considerations are relevant when the figure is to be submitted to a journal requiring APA Style:

■ Authors should read and follow the guidelines for figure preparation in the sixth edition of the *Publication Manual.*

■ Text in a figure can be single-, one-and-a-half-, or double-spaced. Text in the figure caption should be double-spaced.

■ Each figure appears on its own page with its figure caption. All figures should be placed at the end of the manuscript after any tables.

■ Shadings should be easily distinguishable from one another and able to be clearly reduced and reproduced. APA prefers no more than three shadings within the same figure (e.g., for a bar graph, one bar could be white, a second gray, and the third black).

■ Text within the figure should be set in a *sans-serif* font (letters with no cross bars at their tips, usually Helvetica or Arial) to make it easier to read. The text of the figure caption should be in the same font as the text in the rest of the manuscript.

■ The font sizes within the figure should not differ from one another by more than 4 points. Also, the smallest recommended font size is 8 points and the largest recommended font size is 14 points.

■ Labels should be parallel to their respective axes (although labels are sometimes placed perpendicular or at an angle for space considerations).

It is important to note that most of the figures in this book are compliant with APA Style guidelines. When this was not possible, we have made this clear (e.g., when more than three shadings were used in a figure). The APA Style guidelines are useful in creating standards and thus making graphs easier and quicker to read and making the publication process smoother. However, if the venue for a paper is not an APA journal, it is always important to determine the relevant guidelines and standards. When researchers present figures for a report, dissertation, or thesis, they may have much more flexibility about the size of figure. For instance, it is not uncommon to find a figure (e.g., bar graph or line graph) occupying the space of an entire sheet of paper for a thesis. This is less common in a journal, where space limitations are a great concern.

Guidelines for Figure Legends

If a legend is required, usually to define line styles, data point symbols, or shading used to differentiate data sets, a few guidelines need to be followed:

- Incorporate the legend into the body of the figure image (i.e., if any axes are present, place the legend within their boundaries wherever there is white space). If the legend is located outside the body of the image, thus enlarging its dimensions, the figure will need to be reduced more to fit the space available. Following this guideline will ensure that the figure will be reduced as little as possible and will better retain its clarity and legibility.
- Use the same font as in the rest of the figure.
- Capitalize major words in the legend.
- Clearly identify and define each element that needs explanation (e.g., line styles, data point symbols, and shading variants).

Guidelines for Figure Captions

Figure captions consist of a figure number (e.g., Figure 1, Figure 3) and a short description of the figure. The following guidelines should be followed in preparing figure captions:

- Briefly describe the figure. Highlight the important elements of the figure.
- Explain any abbreviations used within the figure that are not identified in the legend of the figure. (If possible, avoid using abbreviations within the figure to facilitate easy reading of the figure.)
- If standard error bars or confidence intervals are included in the figure, explain this in the caption.
- Include sample sizes, statistics used, and probability levels as necessary.
- Type figure captions in the same font as that used in the text of the manuscript. This should be a *serif* font (i.e., the letters have crossbars at their tips) such as Times New Roman.
- The figure caption should be double-spaced.

Guidelines for Placement of Figures and Captions

Use the following APA guidelines for placement of figures in a manuscript:

- Place the image and caption on the same page. See Figures 1.2 and 1.3 for examples. If figure and caption do not fit on the same page, place the caption on a separate page after the figure.

- If there is more than one figure, place each figure on a separate page.
- For manuscript preparation, although the figure number will be identified in the text of the manuscript, many journals require that the figures be included at the end of the manuscript (after the references, author notes, footnotes, and tables). It is common when preparing a figure for a thesis or report to incorporate the figure and caption into the text of the manuscript as soon as possible after the figure has been mentioned in the text; however, it is important to follow guidelines for figure placement specified by the department and/or university.

■ **Checklist of Effective Elements for All Figures**

☐ All text in the figure uses the same style font (sans serif).

☐ All text in the figure is single-spaced, one-and-a-half-spaced, or double-spaced.

☐ Font sizes within a figure do not vary by more than 4 points.

☐ The smallest font size is not less than 8 points, and the largest font size is not greater than 14 points.

☐ Text in the figure caption uses the same font as the text of the manuscript.

☐ The figure caption is double-spaced.

☐ Figure captions are descriptive (i.e., they describe the variables of interest and other important information, such as what abbreviations and symbols mean) and include a permission credit line if the figure was published elsewhere.

☐ Figure captions are presented on the same page as the figure.

☐ Lines in the figure are thick enough to be clear after reduction.

☐ Similar figures within the same manuscript have a similar appearance.

☐ Figures are referred to in the text using the figure number.

Additional Resources

Bigwood, S., & Spore, M. (2003). *Presenting numbers, tables, and charts.* New York, NY: Oxford University Press.

Bowen, R. W. (1992). *Graph it! How to make, read, and interpret graphs.* Englewood Cliffs, NJ: Prentice Hall.

Bar Graphs

What Type of Data Is Presented?

Bar graphs (sometimes referred to as *column graphs*) are useful in presenting or comparing differences between groups. Sometimes they are used to show how groups differ over time. They are also useful for illustrating differences between categorical variables. Although a minimum of two bars is required, it is best to use this type of figure when four or more bars are to be presented.

Example 2.1

A group of researchers wished to examine the hand-gesturing style of men and women. Participants were asked to tell a joke while they were being videotaped for 5 min. The number of large gestures, small gestures, single-hand gestures, and two-hand gestures were counted by three independent judges. Interrater reliability was high enough to average the three judges' total scores (see Figures 2.1–2.8).

Variables for Example 2.1

Independent Variable

1. Gender (male, female)

Dependent Variables

1. Number of large hand gestures
2. Number of small hand gestures
3. Number of one-hand gestures
4. Number of two-hand gestures

Figure 2.1.

The value of the dependent variable is most frequently placed on the *y*-axis (vertical axis).

The *y*-axis to *x*-axis length ratio should be appropriate (e.g., the *y*-axis should be from two thirds to three quarters the length of the *x*-axis).

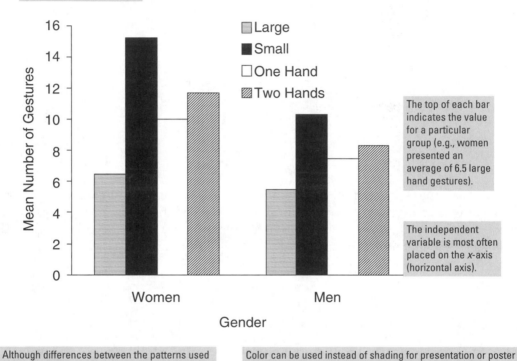

The top of each bar indicates the value for a particular group (e.g., women presented an average of 6.5 large hand gestures).

The independent variable is most often placed on the *x*-axis (horizontal axis).

Although differences between the patterns used to identify the bars may be observable on the computer monitor, when printed they may be indistinguishable. The appearance of the shading can best be verified by checking a laser printout.

Color can be used instead of shading for presentation or poster materials to differentiate the bars. Journal or department and university guidelines need to be verified to determine whether figures are published with color, whether these are placed online only, and what the file specifications are.

Figure X. Average number of times different types of hand gestures were used by women (*n* = 20) and men (*n* = 20) when telling a joke over a 5-min period.

Figure 2.2.

In this version of the figure, the numerical values for the dependent variable are provided above the top of each bar.

The legend should be placed within the boundaries of the axes so that the figure requires as little reduction as possible.

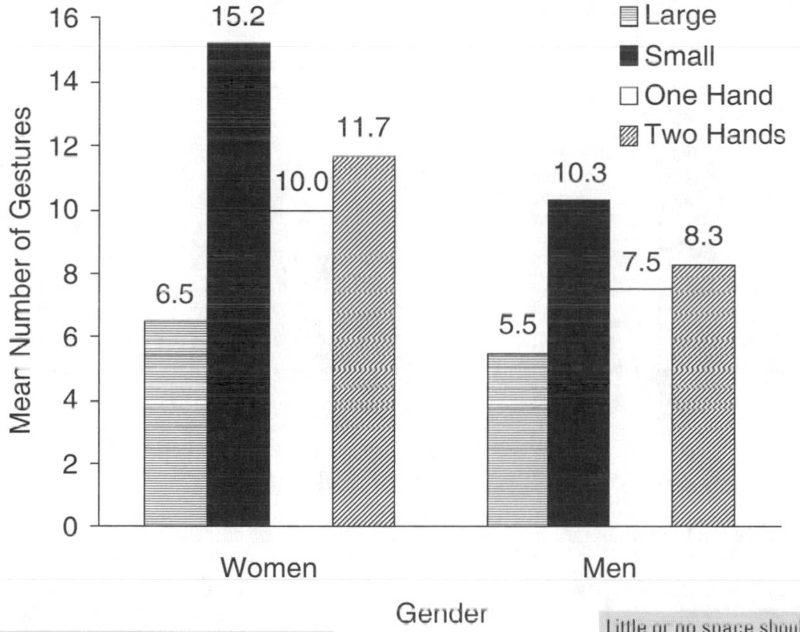

The larger space between the *Women* and *Men* bars and the shorter space on either end of the *x*-axis help readers visually group the bars.

Little or no space should separate bars grouped within one level of the independent variable (e.g., the four bars within *Women*). Large spaces would make the graph not only larger but more difficult to read.

Figure X. Average number of times different types of hand gestures were used by women (*n* = 20) and men (*n* = 20) when telling a joke over a 5-min period.

Figure 2.3.

This version of the figure includes standard error bars.

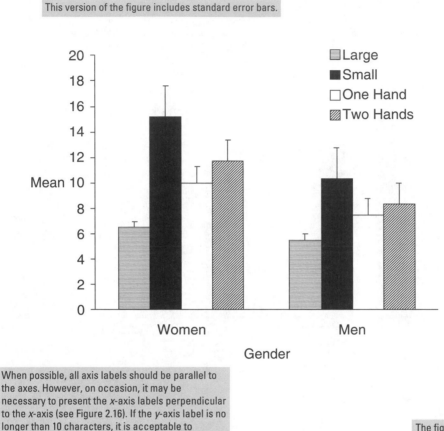

When possible, all axis labels should be parallel to the axes. However, on occasion, it may be necessary to present the x-axis labels perpendicular to the x-axis (see Figure 2.16). If the y-axis label is no longer than 10 characters, it is acceptable to present the label perpendicular to the y-axis, as in the example above.

The figure caption identifies the error bars as standard error bars.

Figure X. Average number of times (±*SE*) different types of hand gestures were used by women (*n* = 20) and men (*n* = 20) when telling a joke over a 5-min period.

◼ **Figure 2.4.**

When double-sided error bars are used, they should be clearly observable on both ends for each of the bars. (They may not be apparent when very dark shading is used.)

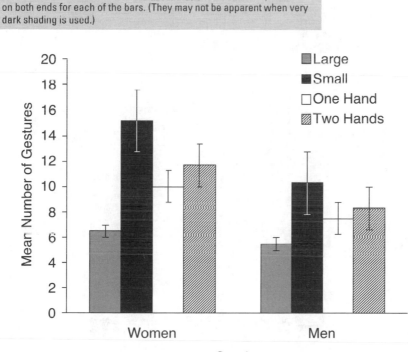

Figure X. Average number of times (±*SE*) different types of hand gestures were used by women (*n* = 20) and men (*n* = 20) when telling a joke over a 5-min period.

The caption specifies the sample size and identifies the error bars as standard error bars.

Figure 2.5.

The bars within the same category are slightly separated from one another to help readers distinguish one bar from another. These spaces should be kept small, however, because large spaces would make the graph more difficult to read. Large spaces should be used only to distinguish different levels of an independent variable (e.g., *Women* and *Men*).

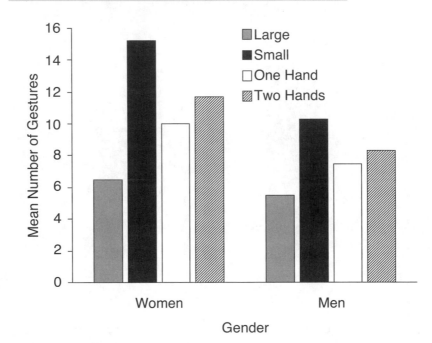

Figure X. Average number of times different types of hand gestures were used by women (*n* = 20) and men (*n* = 20) when telling a joke over a 5-min period.

Figure 2.6.

This graph is sometimes referred to as a *stacked bar graph*. It permits the reader to make comparisons between overall frequencies but makes comparisons between bars more difficult.

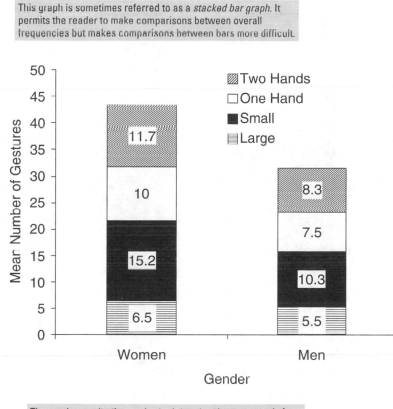

The *y*-axis permits the reader to determine the mean totals for each bar as well as compare the individual means with the total mean. Because it is more difficult to estimate the values of the stacked bars, exact values should be provided within the bars.

Figure X. Average number of times different hand gestures were used by women (*n* = 20) and men (*n* = 20) when telling a joke over a 5-min period.

Figure 2.7.

Three-dimensional graphs may appear sophisticated, but they are considerably more difficult to read. It is best to keep graphs simple and avoid special effects that are visually distracting.

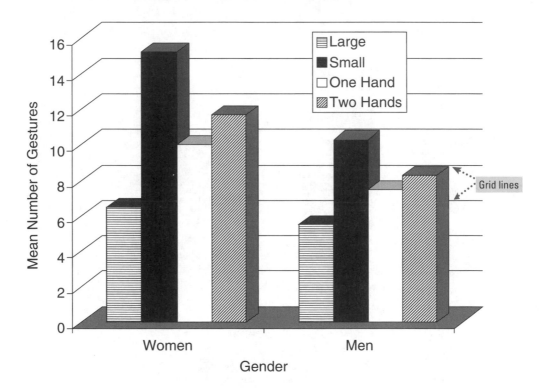

Figure X. Average number of times different types of hand gestures were used by women (*n* = 20) and men (*n* = 20) when telling a joke over a 5-min period.

Grid lines, which can make the *y*-axis values easier to read, especially in figures that are wider than this one (i.e., figures with a very long *x*-axis), are provided here. Some journals prefer to eliminate the grid lines.

▨ Figure 2.8.

If the bar graph is getting too tall and all of the results are greater than 0, the y-axis may start at a value other than 0. The two diagonal lines on the y-axis alert the reader that the y-axis does not start at 0. Differences between groups may appear exaggerated when a y-axis break is introduced.

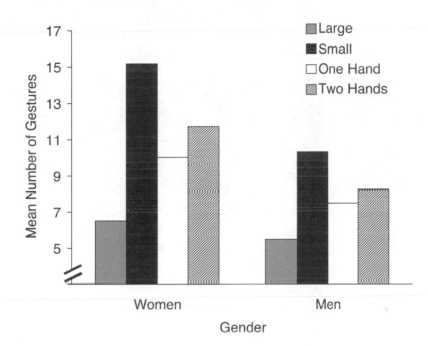

Figure X. Average number of times different types of hand gestures were used by women (*n* = 20) and men (*n* = 20) when telling a joke over a 5-min period.

Example 2.2

The same researchers wished to compare the hand-gesturing styles of 20-year-old and 60-year-old men and women telling a joke. Participants were given a script to memorize and asked to tell the story to another person while being videotaped. (The other person was the experimenters' accomplice, who was asked to react in a similar manner for all of the participants.) The numbers of large and small gestures were counted by two independent judges and averaged (interrater reliability indicated that averaging their scores was warranted). Figure 2.9 presents the results.

Variables for Example 2.2

Independent Variables

1. Gender (male, female)
2. Age (20 years old, 60 years old)

Dependent Variables

1. Number of large hand gestures
2. Number of small hand gestures

■ **Figure 2.9.**

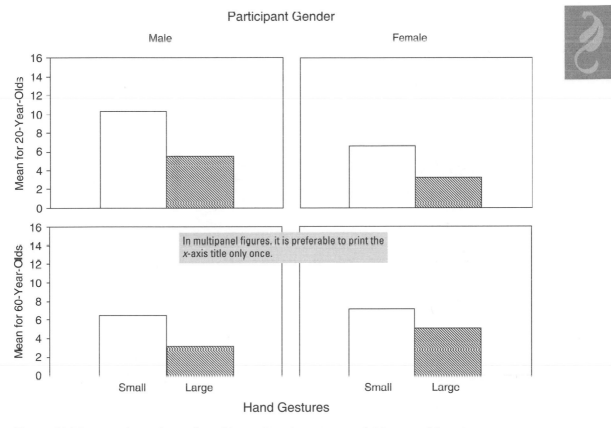

Participant Gender

Figure X. The number of small and large hand gestures of 20-year-old and 60-year-old men and women when telling a joke.

Four graphs were created and placed together in a single figure.

Example 2.3

Two researchers wished to determine the extent to which hand gestures in early life match hand gestures later in life. One hundred and fifty 5-year-old children were classified into one of two groups: (a) many hand gestures present or (b) few hand gestures present. Fifteen years later, these individuals were asked to allow a close friend to complete a paper-and-pencil measure to assess the extent to which they used a variety of hand gestures. The 20-year-olds were rated on the extent to which they used *inclusive* (draws other people into a conversation), *exclusive* (excludes other people from a conversation), relevant, and irrelevant hand gestures. Figure 2.10 presents the results.

Variables for Example 2.3

Independent Variable

1. Age (5 years old, 20 years old)

Dependent Variables

1. Hand gestures at age 5 (many, few)
2. Hand gestures at age 20 (inclusive, exclusive, relevant, irrelevant)

Figure 2.10.

In figures where more than one graph is presented, if the legend is identical for the two graphs, it is presented only once in the first or top graph.

This figure illustrates one way of presenting negative values.

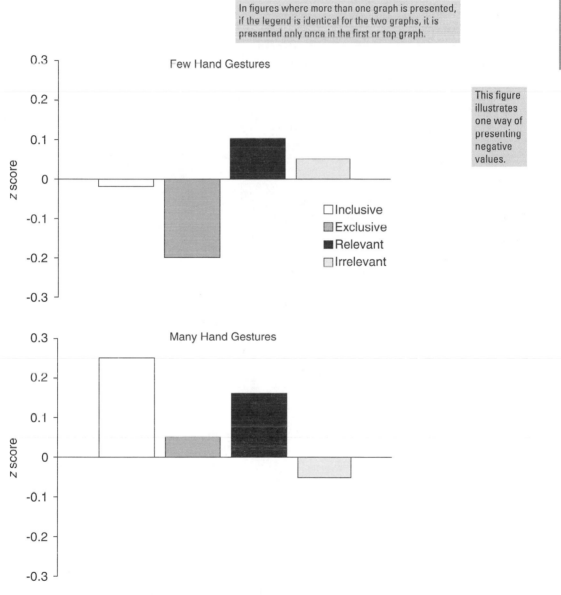

Figure X. Age 5 hand gesture behavior (few or many gestures) and the same participants' scores at age 20 on a hand gesture survey (inclusive, exclusive, relevant, irrelevant) as rated by a close peer. The figure shows *z* scores (*M* = 0, *SD* = 1) standardized on the full sample.

Example 2.4

A researcher sought to determine whether a performance goal oriented training program, a learning goal oriented training program, or a subject-based goal oriented training program was better than the traditional training program used at a college to teach young adults about first aid. Individuals were placed in one of the four experimental conditions. Their results on a written test were then compared in Figures 2.11–2.15.

Variables for Example 2.4

Independent Variable

1. Type of training program (traditional, performance, learning, subject-based)

Dependent Variable

1. Score on a written test

■ **Figure 2.11.**

An asterisk can be used in bar graphs to indicate significance levels. The asterisk presented over the performance condition indicates that post hoc differences were found between that condition and each of the other groups. No intergroup differences were found for the traditional, learning, and subject-based groups.

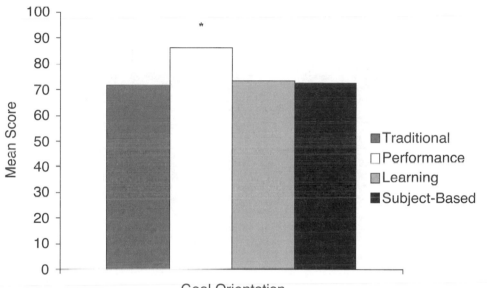

Figure X. Mean test scores for participants in the traditional (*n* = 22), performance (*n* = 21), learning (*n* = 17), and subject-based (*n* = 19) goal oriented groups. *p < .01.

The asterisk in the figure must be described in the figure caption.

Figure 2.12.

Letters can be used in bar graphs to indicate significance levels for comparisons. When bars share the same letters, they show no significant differences from one another. Bars with different letters show significant differences.

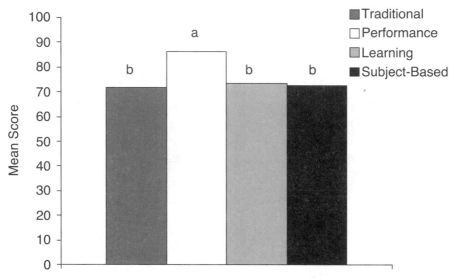

Figure X. Mean test scores for participants in the traditional (*n* = 22), performance (*n* = 21), learning (*n* = 17), and subject-based (*n* = 19) goal oriented groups. Bars sharing the same letter do not differ significantly from each other. Significant differences are at *p* < .01.

The meaning of the letters presented over the bars in the figure must be described in the figure caption.

Figure 2.13.

Another way to illustrate significance of comparisons is with the use of lines that link the groups that are significantly different from one another.

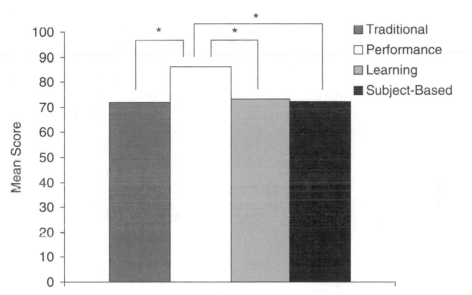

Figure X. Mean test scores for participants in the traditional ($n = 22$), performance ($n = 21$), learning ($n - 17$), and subject-based ($n = 19$) goal oriented groups. *$p < .01$.

The exact p values can be presented in the graph above the lines (instead of the asterisk). (For more on reporting p values, see sections 4.35 and 5.16 of the sixth edition of the *Publication Manual.*)

Figure 2.14.

Figure X. Mean test scores for participants in the traditional (*n* = 22), performance (*n* = 21), learning (*n* = 17), and subject-based (*n* = 19) goal oriented groups.

Figure 2.15.

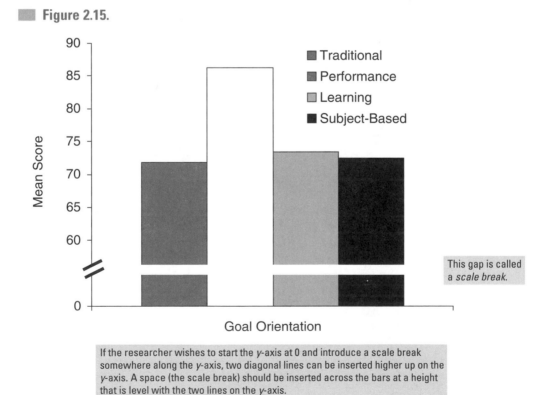

Figure X. Mean test scores for participants in the traditional (*n* = 22), performance (*n* = 21), learning (*n* = 17), and subject-based (*n* = 19) goal oriented groups.

Example 2.5

A researcher wished to determine whether individuals in various traditional professions felt fulfilled and had a sense of the meaning of life. He obtained nominal lists of accountants, administrative assistants, garment workers, cooks, dentists, general practitioners, graduate students, high-level managers, low-level managers, maintenance (cleaning) engineers, mechanics, clergy, nurses, professors, sales clerks, servers, and taxi drivers. He sent each person on his list a fulfillment/meaning of life survey. He obtained a 30% response rate and compared the responses by trade, as shown in Figure 2.16.

Variables for Example 2.5

Independent Variable

1. Trade (accountant, administrative assistant, garment worker, cook, dentist, general practitioner, graduate student, high-level manager, low-level manager, maintenance engineer, mechanic, clergy, nurse, professor, sales clerk, server, taxi driver)

Dependent Variable

1. Fulfillment/meaning of life score

Figure 2.16.

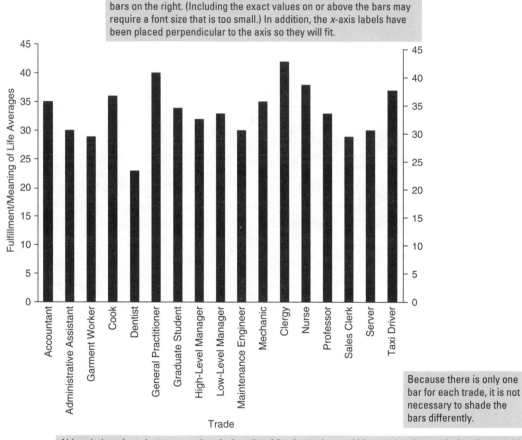

Because of the large number of bars, a second *y*-axis has been included on the right of this graph to make it easier to estimate the values of the bars on the right. (Including the exact values on or above the bars may require a font size that is too small.) In addition, the *x*-axis labels have been placed perpendicular to the axis so they will fit.

Because there is only one bar for each trade, it is not necessary to shade the bars differently.

Abbreviations (e.g., letter or number designations) for the trades could be used on the *x*-axis, but they would require explanation in the figure caption. This should be done only when necessary; looking back and forth from the figure to the caption to determine what each bar represents is an inconvenience for readers.

Figure X. Average scores on the fulfillment/meaning of life scale for the 17 professions studied.

Example 2.6

Three researchers were studying whether men's and women's feelings of fulfillment were the same at various ages. The researchers asked men and women of various age groups to complete a fulfillment/meaning of life survey. The age groups they studied were 20–29, 30–39, 40–49, 50–59, 60–69, and 70–79 years. They presented their results in Figure 2.17.

Variables for Example 2.6

Independent Variables

1. Gender (female, male)
2. Age category (20–29, 30–39, 40–49, 50–59, 60–69, 70–79)

Dependent Variable

1. Fulfillment/meaning of life score

Figure 2.17.

| The dependent variable is on the *x*-axis and not on the *y*-axis in this example. | This is an example of an upside-down pyramid graph. It is not frequently used because it is preferable to put the dependent variable on the *y*-axis rather than on the *x*-axis. Nevertheless, comparisons are easy to make when this form of graph is used. |

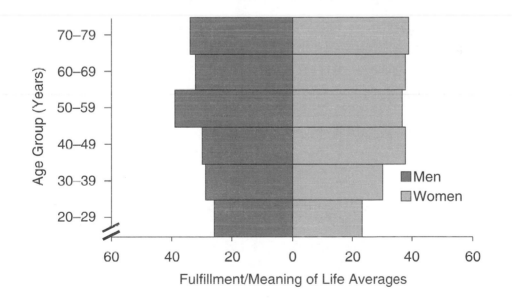

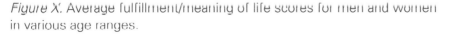

Figure X. Average fulfillment/meaning of life scores for men and women in various age ranges.

▨ Checklist of Effective Elements for Bar Graphs

☐ In axis labels and titles, the first letter of the first word and all major words are capitalized.

☐ In legends, the first letter of the first word and all major words are capitalized.

☐ The dependent variable is on the vertical (y) axis (unless there is a reason to put it on the x-axis).

☐ The independent variable is on the horizontal (x) axis (unless there is a reason to put it on the y-axis).

☐ The y-axis/x-axis length ratio is appropriate (usually, the y-axis should be two thirds to three fourths the length of the x-axis).

☐ Axes are clearly labeled.

☐ Axis labels are parallel to the axes, if possible.

☐ Positive values on the x-axis increase to the right, whereas those on the y-axis increase up.

☐ Negative values on the x-axis increase to the left, whereas those on the y-axis increase down.

☐ The highest values on the x-axis and y-axis scales are larger than the highest data values (i.e., the x- and y-axes are longer than the area covered by the largest data values).

☐ Bars representing different independent variables within the graph can be clearly differentiated from one another.

☐ Bars are of the same width.

☐ In multipanel figures (a figure with two or more graphs), the legend and the x-axis title are printed only once if they are identical across all of the graphs. The x-axis title is usually presented on the bottom graph and the legend on the top graph.

Histograms

3

What Type of Data Is Presented?

Histograms are illustrations of frequency distributions in which bars of different heights are use to represent observed frequencies. In histograms, the x-axis presents the categories by which the data have been classified (usually quantitative variables such as weight, height, age, year). It is important that the variable on the x-axis starts small and ends large (going small to large from left to right) so that the shape of the distribution can be easily discerned.

Example 3.1

One teaching assistant of a sociology course had completed marking the midterm exams and wished to present the results in a histogram for the students. The grades were grouped as follows: 0–10, 11–20, 21–30, 31–40, 41–50, 51–60, 61–70, 71–80, 81–90, 91–100. A sample histogram for the results is presented in Figure 3.1.

Variable for Example 3.1

1. Grade

Figure 3.1.

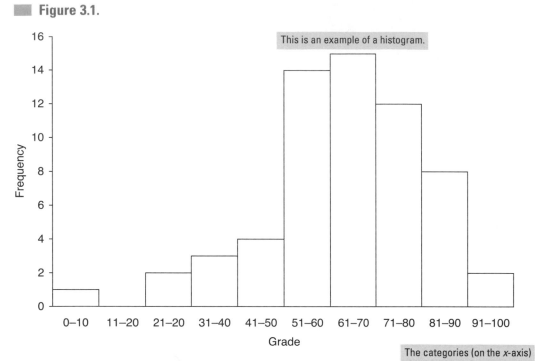

Figure X. Test scores for students in Sociology 101.

▨ Checklist of Effective Elements for Histograms

☐ In axis labels and titles, the first letter of the first word and all major words are capitalized.

☐ In legends, the first letter of the first word and all major words are capitalized.

☐ The frequency distribution is on the vertical (y) axis.

☐ The independent variable is on the horizontal (x) axis.

☐ The y-axis/x-axis length ratio is appropriate (usually, the y-axis should be two thirds to three fourths the length of the x-axis).

☐ Axes are clearly labeled.

☐ Axis labels are parallel to the axes, if possible.

☐ Positive values on the x-axis increase to the right, whereas those on the y-axis increase up.

☐ The highest values on the x-axis and y-axis scales are larger than the highest data values (i.e., the x- and y-axes are longer than the area covered by the largest data values).

☐ Bars are of the same width and touch each other on the x-axis.

☐ In multipanel figures (a figure with two or more graphs), the legend and the x-axis title are printed only once if they are identical across all of the graphs. The x-axis title is usually presented on the bottom graph and the legend on the top graph.

4

Line Graphs

What Type of Data Is Presented?

A line graph is used to present a change in one or more dependent variables as a function of an independent variable. It is particularly useful in demonstrating a trend or an interaction. Types of data effectively presented using a line graph include average changes in scores for the dependent variable over time, trials, or some other independent variable and average correlations over trials or time.

A line graph figure must have at least three data points. It is much more common to see four points (particularly to present interaction effects) or even up to 10 points in a single-line graph.

Example 4.1

A senior undergraduate student wrote 30 items that she hoped would form a new measure of naiveté. As part of the validation study, she conducted a principal-components analysis to determine the factor structure of the measure. In her thesis she presented a *scree plot* (which shows the proportion of variance that is accounted for by the individual factors) to illustrate the number of factors in her measure (Figure 4.1).

Variable for Example 4.1

1. Thirty items of the naiveté questionnaire

■ Figure 4.1.

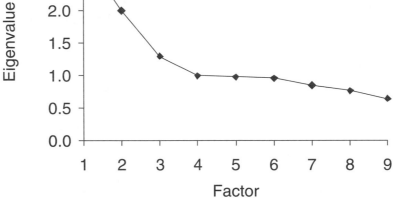

Figure X. Scree plot of the measure of naiveté.

Example 4.2

A student was interested in learning whether the topic of industrial/organizational (I/O) psychology was perceived by graduate students to be covered in introductory psychology textbooks more now than in the past. She asked graduate students to estimate the number of pages devoted to I/O psychology in the typical introductory psychology textbooks published between 1950 and 2010. She presented the results in a line graph (see Figures 4.2–4.5).

Variables for Example 4.2

Independent Variable

1. Year introductory psychology textbook was published (1950–2010)

Dependent Variable

1. Estimates of the number of pages devoted to I/O psychology in introductory psychology textbooks each year

---

■ **Figure 4.2.**

It is better for axis labels to be concise enough to fit on one line, though they can be longer, as shown here.

The dependent variable is on the *y*-axis (vertical axis).

The *y*-axis should be from two thirds to three fourths the length of the *x*-axis (horizontal axis).

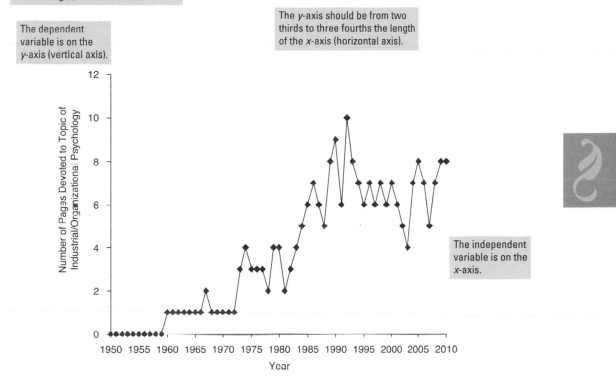

The independent variable is on the *x*-axis.

Figure X. Mean estimates by graduate students of the number of pages devoted to industrial/organizational psychology in introductory psychology textbooks published between 1950 and 2010.

The caption should be descriptive enough so that readers do not have to refer to the text to understand the graph.

■■■ **Figure 4.3.**

This figure illustrates why data points should be highlighted using a small character such as a square or a circle to help the reader read the graph more accurately. Note how in this figure the values for years not labeled on the x-axis are more difficult to discern than they are in Figure 4.2.

Although it is preferable to present all axis labels parallel to the axes, it may be necessary to present numerous x-axis labels angled or perpendicular to the x-axis. Labels for the y-axis no longer than 10 characters may also be perpendicular.

Figure X. Mean estimates by graduate students of the number of pages devoted to industrial/organizational psychology in introductory psychology textbooks published between 1950 and 2010.

Figure 4.4.

In this figure, some of the data points are labeled to facilitate reading the graph.

The font sizes used within a figure should not differ by more than 4 font points.

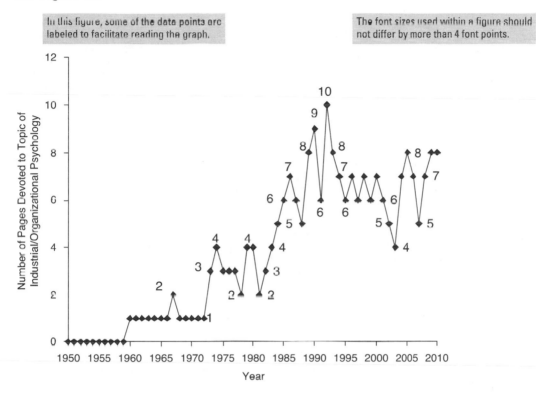

Figure X. Mean estimates by graduate students of the number of pages devoted to industrial/organizational psychology in introductory psychology textbooks published between 1950 and 2010.

■ **Figure 4.5.**

Horizontal grid lines are included to facilitate reading the values on the
y-axis. If grid lines are too close together, they can clutter the figure.
Some journals prefer to eliminate the grid lines.

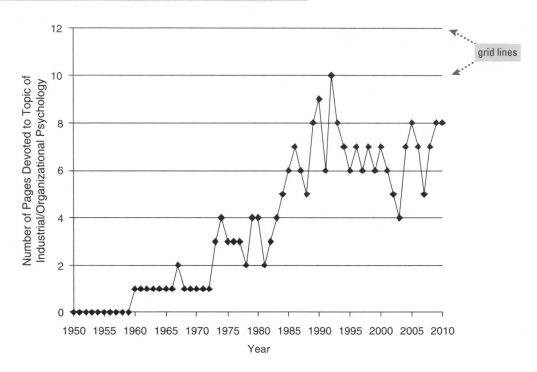

Figure X. Mean estimates by graduate students of the number of pages devoted to industrial/organizational psychology in introductory psychology textbooks published between 1950 and 2010.

Example 4.3

In addition to the estimated number of pages in introductory psychology textbooks that covered topics in I/O psychology, the Example 4.2 student wished to determine the extent to which paranormal psychology was covered in these same books. The same participants were asked to estimate the extent to which their introductory psychology books covered the topic of paranormal psychology. The results are presented in Figure 4.6.

Variables for Example 4.3

Independent Variable

1. Year introductory psychology textbook was published (1950–2010)

Dependent Variables

1. Estimates of the number of pages devoted to I/O psychology in introductory psychology textbooks each year
2. Estimates of the number of pages devoted to paranormal psychology in introductory psychology textbooks each year

Figure 4.6.

When there are two or more lines, changing the line style and data point symbols can make the graph easier to read, especially when the lines overlap or cross.

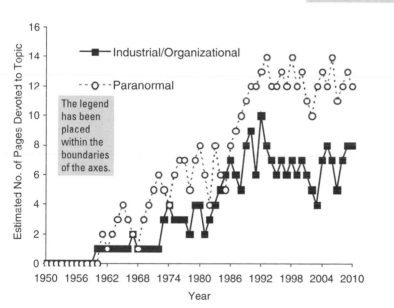

Use simple symbols (squares, circles). Distracting symbols such as stars or happy faces should be avoided.

The legend has been placed within the boundaries of the axes.

Although differences among symbols and lines may be clear on the computer monitor, they may not be visible in printed form. Verify the appearance of symbols and lines by reviewing a black-and-white printout.

Figure X. Mean estimates of the number of pages devoted to industrial/organizational psychology and paranormal psychology in introductory psychology textbooks published between 1950 and 2010.

Color can be used to differentiate lines and symbols for conference presentation or poster materials (see Chapters 13 and 14). However, many academic book and journal publishers do not print color, especially for simple line art. Researchers should first check the journal submission guidelines or university guidelines to determine acceptability and specifications of color figures; some journals publish in color for articles that appear on the web but not in print.

Example 4.4

A researcher wished to determine the effectiveness of a meditation technique in reducing a nervous eye-blinking tic. Two groups of individuals participated: One group had developed an eye-blinking tic within the past year, and the other had had the tic for 5 or more years. The researcher first obtained a series of baseline measures by filming each participant for 1 hr at four separate sessions and counting the number of eye-blinking tics. The average number of eye-blinking tics per 5 min was calculated for each of the four sessions. Then participants were taught to use a deep breathing and relaxation meditation technique. Participants used the technique for 15 min a day for 1 week and then stopped using the technique for 1 week. This cycle was maintained for 8 weeks, with measures of eye-blinking tics taken three times each week (for a total of four baseline measures and 24 experimental measures). Figures 4.7–4.10 illustrate the results.

Variables for Example 4.4

Independent Variables

1. Session—measurement (via 1 hr of filming) of eye-blinking tic three times per week during use or nonuse of a deep breathing and relaxation meditation technique
2. Length of time an eye-blinking tic was present (up to 1 year, 5 or more years)

Dependent Variable

1. Average number of eye-blinking tics in a 5-min period

Figure 4.7.

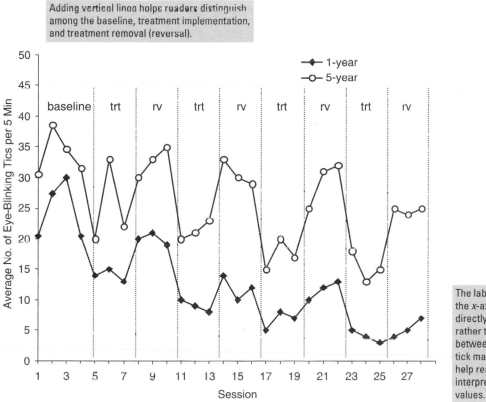

Adding vertical lines helps readers distinguish among the baseline, treatment implementation, and treatment removal (reversal).

The labels on the x-axis are directly under, rather than between, the tick marks to help readers interpret the values.

Figure X. Average number of eye-blinking tics for participants with a tic problem for up to 1 year (*n* = 24) and for participants with a tic problem for a minimum of 5 years (*n* = 18). trt = treatment; rv = reversal.

The figure caption identifies sample sizes and defines abbreviations.

▨ Figure 4.8.

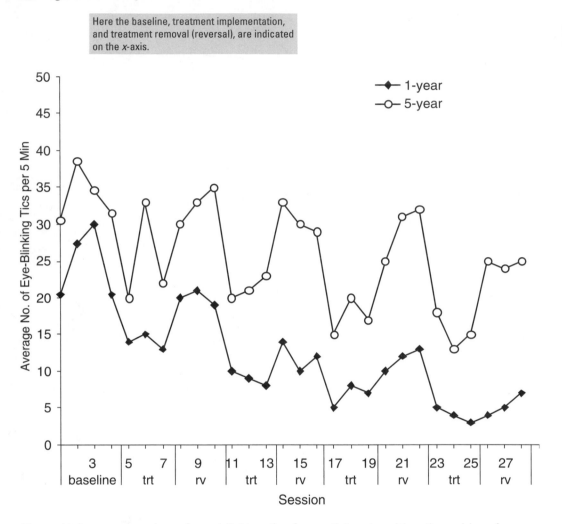

Here the baseline, treatment implementation, and treatment removal (reversal), are indicated on the *x*-axis.

Figure X. Average number of eye-blinking tics for participants with a tic problem for up to 1 year (*n* = 24) and for participants with a tic problem for a minimum of 5 years (*n* = 18). trt = treatment; rv = reversal.

Figure 4.9.

The various treatment effects are indicated by including gaps between them. (The line forming the x-axis may be continued, rather than incorporating actual spaces.)

The legend has been boxed to set it apart from other elements in the graph.

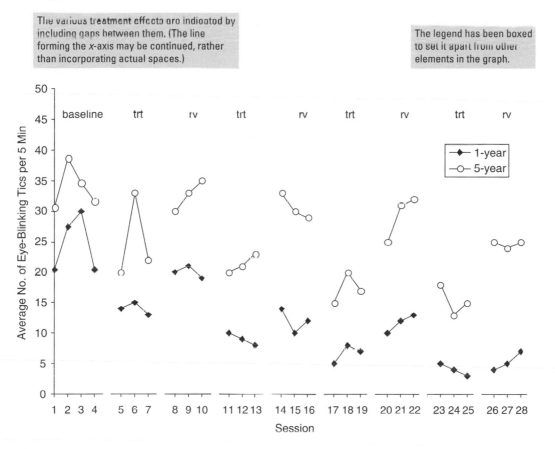

Figure X. Average number of eye-blinking tics for participants with this problem for up to 1 year (*n* = 24) and for participants with this problem for a minimum of 5 years (*n* = 18). trt = treatment; rv = reversal.

Figure 4.10.

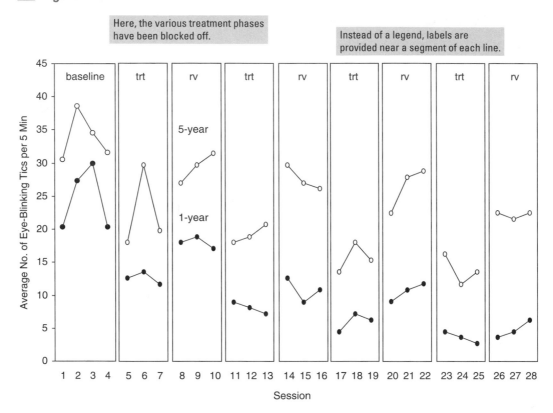

Figure X. Average number of eye-blinking tics for participants with a tic problem for up to 1 year (*n* = 24) and for participants with a tic problem for a minimum of 5 years (*n* = 18). trt = treatment; rv = reversal.

Example 4.5

The Example 4.4 researcher wished to determine whether participants in the eye-blinking tic study would continue to demonstrate lower levels of tics after a 6-month delay. He obtained baseline measures again and measures after two treatments and one reversal. To compare the results with the earlier study, he could choose to include all of the results in a single graph (Figure 4.11) or in two graphs within one figure (Figure 4.12).

Variables for Example 4.5

Independent Variables

1. Session—measurement (via 1 hr of filming) of eye-blinking tic three times per week following use or nonuse of a deep breathing and relaxation meditation technique
2. Length of time an eye-blinking tic was present (up to 1 year, 5 or more years)

Dependent Variable

1. Average number of eye-blinking tics in a 5-min period

 Figure 4.11.

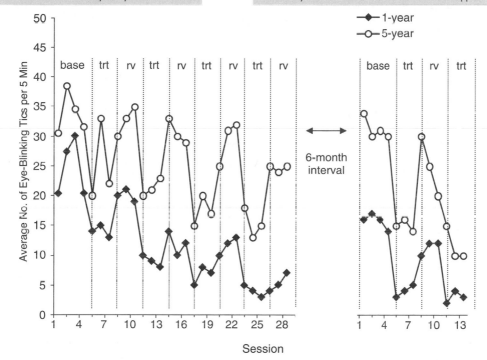

Presenting a break in the graph (at the *x*-axis) and including both sets of data in a single graph allows the reader to easily compare the results.

Sometimes it is not possible to label each tick mark on the *x*-axis. Readers should be able to extrapolate the units denoted by the tick marks from the values that appear.

Figure X. Average number of eye-blinking tics for participants with a tic problem for up to 1 year (*n* = 24) and for participants with a tic problem for a minimum of 5 years (*n* = 18). Eye-blinking tics were counted at baseline and over an 8-week period of alternating introduction and reversal of the treatment. After 6 months, baseline measures and treatment and reversal were implemented again (*n* = 19 for the 1-year sample, *n* = 10 for the 5-year sample). base = baseline; trt = treatment; rv = reversal.

Figure 4.12.

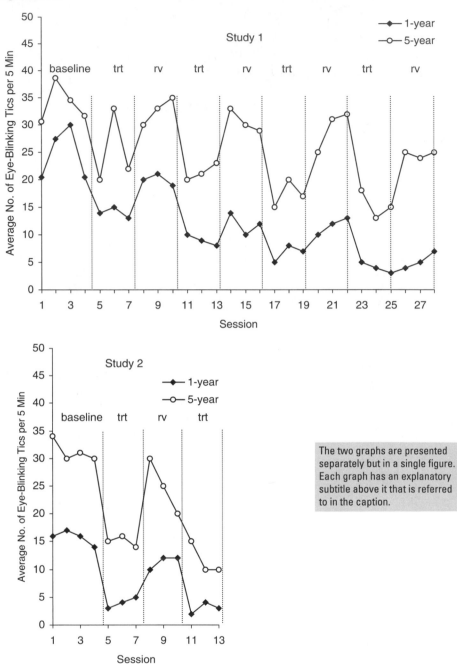

The two graphs are presented separately but in a single figure. Each graph has an explanatory subtitle above it that is referred to in the caption.

Figure X. Average number of eye-blinking tics for participants with a tic problem for up to 1 year (*n* = 24) and for participants with a tic problem for a minimum of 5 years (*n* = 18). In Study 1, eye-blinking tics were counted at baseline and over an 8-week period of alternating introduction and reversal of the treatment. After 6 months, baseline measures and treatment and reversal were implemented again for Study 2 (*n* = 19 for the 1-year sample, *n* = 10 for the 5-year sample). trt = treatment; rv = reversal.

Example 4.6

The Example 4.4 researcher sought to determine the effectiveness of an exercise program on the reduction of an eye-blinking tic. As in Example 4.4, two groups of individuals participated: One group had developed an eye-blinking tic within the past year, and the other had had the tic for 5 or more years. The researcher first obtained three baseline measures of the number of eye-blinking tics and calculated the average number of eye tics per 5 min for each of the three measures. The individuals then participated in a 1-hr aerobics class every 3 days and refrained from extensive physical activity at other times. Measures of eye-blinking tics were taken every day. A total of six aerobics classes were given. Figures 4.13–4.15 illustrate various ways the results could be displayed.

Variables for Example 4.6

Independent Variables

1. Aerobics classes
2. The length of time an eye-blinking tic was present (1 year, 5 or more years)

Dependent Variable

1. Average number of eye-blinking tics in a 5-min period

■ **Figure 4.13.**

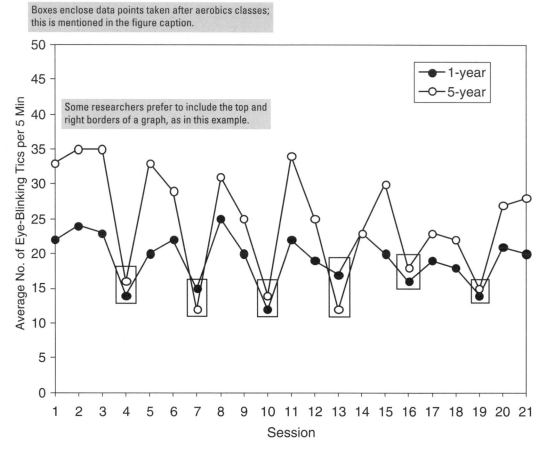

Figure X. Average number of eye-blinking tics for participants with a tic problem for up to 1 year (*n* = 17) and for participants with a tic problem for a minimum of 5 years (*n* = 15). Boxes enclose measures taken immediately after an aerobics class.

Figure 4.14.

Standard error bars are
included in this figure.

The standard error bars in
the graph are identified
as such in the caption.

The lines are defined using arrows instead
of a legend.

The treatment sessions are indicated by
x-axis labels in boldface. (The figure
caption explains the use of boldface.)

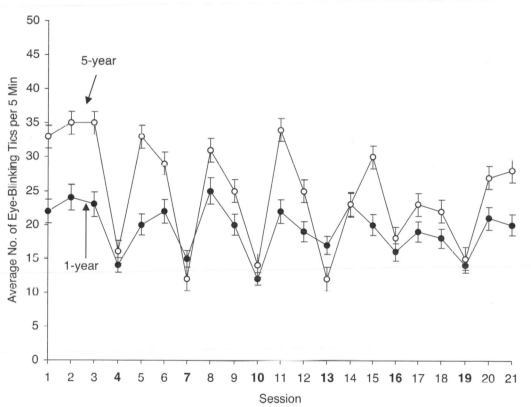

Figure X. Average number of eye-blinking tics for participants with a tic problem for
up to 1 year (*n* = 17; black circles) and for participants with a tic problem for a minimum
of 5 years (*n* = 15; white circles). Standard errors are also provided. Boldface axis labels
denote measures taken immediately after an aerobics class.

Figure 4.15.

If all of the results are greater than 0, the *y*-axis may start at a value greater than 0 to conserve space. Two diagonal lines are inserted on the *y*-axis to alert the reader that the *y*-axis does not start at 0.

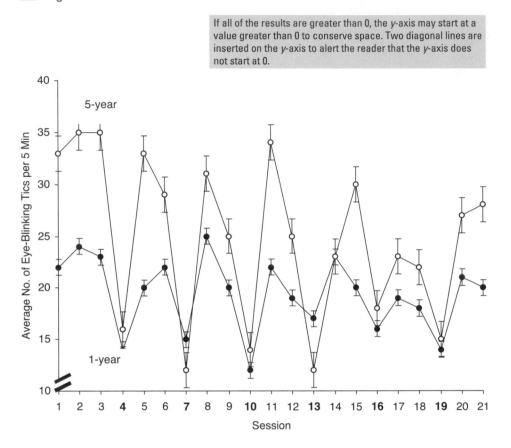

Figure X. Average number of eye-blinking tics for participants with a tic problem for up to 1 year (*n* = 17; black circles) and for participants with a tic problem for a minimum of 5 years (*n* = 15; white circles). Standard errors are also provided. Labels for the *x*-axis in boldface denote measures taken immediately after an aerobics class.

Example 4.7

Three researchers wished to examine the effects of stress and violent television on 8-year-old children. Stress was operationalized as the anticipation of an upcoming exam (high stress) or the absence of an upcoming exam (low stress). The violent television programs consisted of two animation shows shown on a cable network station on Saturday mornings (independent raters rated the two shows for violence prior to the commencement of the study). Children who participated did not have access to this cable network, and their parents permitted them to take part in the study.

The researchers developed a 2 × 2 experimental design whereby participants were placed in one of four conditions: (a) high stress and high TV violence, (b) low stress and high TV violence, (c) high stress and low TV violence, and (d) low stress and low TV violence. The researchers wished to determine whether there was an effect on children's aggressive behavior (children were filmed and their behavior coded by independent raters). Furthermore, the researchers wished to determine whether there was an interaction effect between the two independent variables. Figure 4.16 presents their results.

Variables for Example 4.7

Independent Variables

1. Stress (high, low)
2. Violence (high, low)

Dependent Variable

1. Aggression

Figure 4.16.

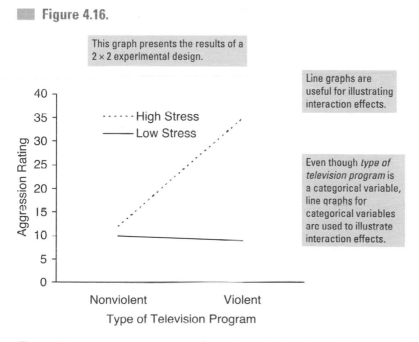

This graph presents the results of a 2 × 2 experimental design.

Line graphs are useful for illustrating interaction effects.

Even though *type of television program* is a categorical variable, line graphs for categorical variables are used to illustrate interaction effects.

Figure X. Aggression level as a function of television violence and level of stress in a sample of forty 8-year-old children, with 10 children per condition.

Example 4.8

The Example 4.7 researchers wished to determine whether there was a $2 \times 3 \times 2$ (three-way) interaction effect among stress level, television violence, and sugar intake. Stress and violent programming were operationalized in a manner similar to that in Example 4.7, except that an extra condition was added to the violent programming: a moderate violence condition. For the additional independent variable of sugar intake, children were given a drink of either (a) water, flavoring, and sugar or (b) water, flavoring, and artificial sweetener. Figures 4.17–4.20 depict different ways of presenting the results.

Variables for Example 4.8

Independent Variables

1. Stress (low, high)
2. Violence (none, medium, high)
3. Sugar (none, high)

Dependent Variable

1. Aggression

Figure 4.17.

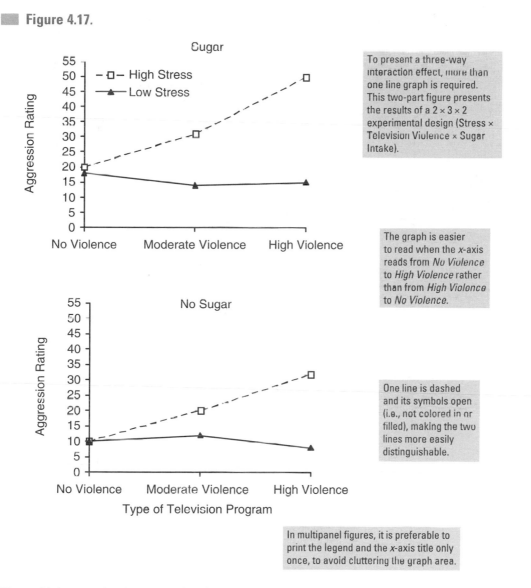

To present a three-way interaction effect, more than one line graph is required. This two-part figure presents the results of a 2 × 3 × 2 experimental design (Stress × Television Violence × Sugar Intake).

The graph is easier to read when the x-axis reads from *No Violence* to *High Violence* rather than from *High Violence* to *No Violence*.

One line is dashed and its symbols open (i.e., not colored in or filled), making the two lines more easily distinguishable.

In multipanel figures, it is preferable to print the legend and the x-axis title only once, to avoid cluttering the graph area.

Figure X. Aggression in a sample of 120 children as a function of stress level, level of violence in a television program, and sugar intake.

Figure 4.18.

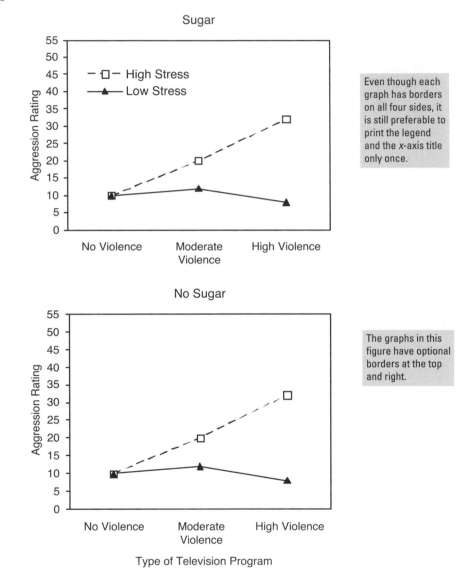

Even though each graph has borders on all four sides, it is still preferable to print the legend and the x-axis title only once.

The graphs in this figure have optional borders at the top and right.

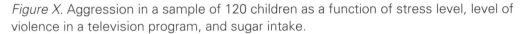

Figure X. Aggression in a sample of 120 children as a function of stress level, level of violence in a television program, and sugar intake.

Figure 4.19.

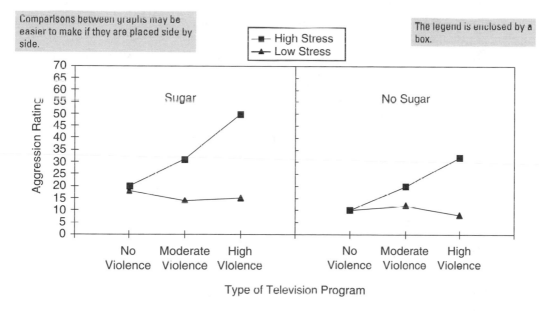

Comparisons between graphs may be easier to make if they are placed side by side.

The legend is enclosed by a box.

Figure X. Aggression in a sample of 120 children as a function of stress level, level of violence in a television program, and sugar intake.

Figure 4.20.

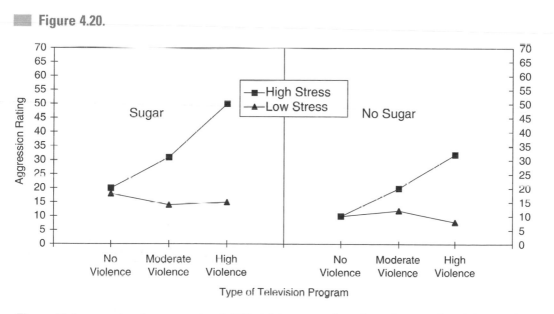

Figure X. Aggression in a sample of 120 children as a function of stress level, level of violence in a television program, and sugar intake.

Example 4.9

The Example 4.8 researchers wished to examine how moderate sugar intake level and moderate stress level would influence the level of aggression in children. There are still three independent variables, but now there are three levels of each independent variable; this is a $3 \times 3 \times 3$ design. Results are presented in Figure 4.21.

Variables for Example 4.9

Independent Variables

1. Stress (low, moderate, high)
2. Violence (none, medium, high)
3. Sugar (none, moderate, high)

Dependent Variable

1. Aggression

Figure 4.21.

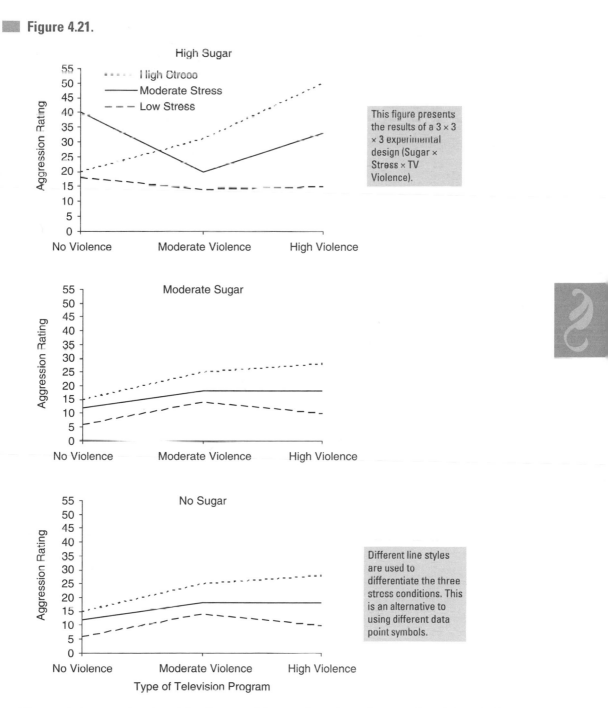

This figure presents the results of a 3 × 3 × 3 experimental design (Sugar × Stress × TV Violence).

Different line styles are used to differentiate the three stress conditions. This is an alternative to using different data point symbols.

Figure X. Aggression level for 8-year-olds as a function of stress level, level of violence in a television program, and level of sugar intake.

If the caption will not fit on the same page as the figure, it should be included on the page following the figure.

Example 4.10

A researcher was interested in the extent to which individuals with depression and individuals without depression are able to determine whether drawn faces are symmetrical. Each participant was tested individually in front of a computer screen that presented the various faces. The participant's task was to indicate, using the keyboard, whether the face presented was symmetrical. Each participant's reaction time and percentage of errors made were recorded by the computer, and Figures 4.22 and 4.23 present the results.

Variables for Example 4.10

Independent Variable

1. Face symmetry (symmetrical, nonsymmetrical)

Dependent Variables

1. Reaction time in milliseconds
2. Percentage of errors made

Figure 4.22.

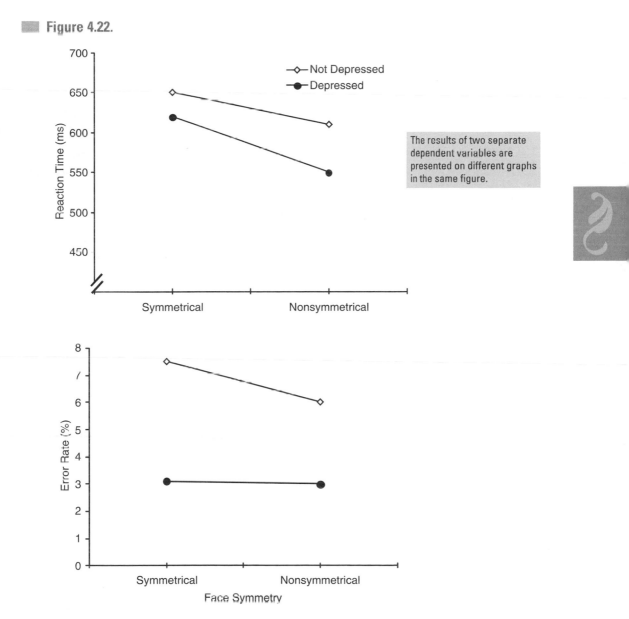

The results of two separate dependent variables are presented on different graphs in the same figure.

Figure X. Reaction times (top) and error rates (bottom) as a function of presence of depression and identification of facial symmetry.

■ **Figure 4.23.**

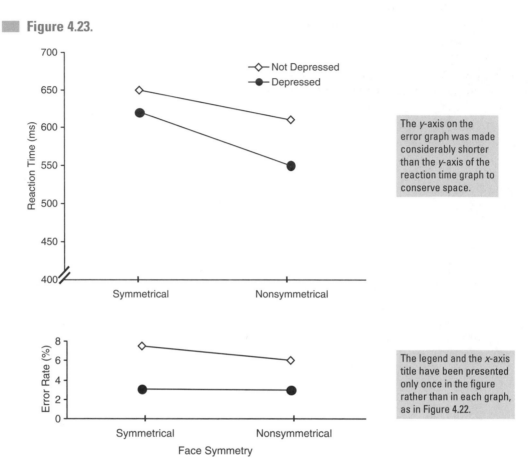

The *y*-axis on the error graph was made considerably shorter than the *y*-axis of the reaction time graph to conserve space.

The legend and the *x*-axis title have been presented only once in the figure rather than in each graph, as in Figure 4.22.

Figure X. Reaction times (top) and error rates (bottom) as a function of presence of depression and identification of facial symmetry.

Example 4.11

A researcher working at a counseling center in a university wished to evaluate the center's test anxiety program. The anxiety program consisted of 2-hr weekly group instruction and counseling sessions for a maximum of 15 individuals for up to 4 weeks. The program was popular and usually had an extensive waiting list.

To conduct a program evaluation with an adequate sample size, the researcher decided to determine the progress of three different groups. Because the groups attended the program in consecutive months, the researcher obtained baseline measures over 2 weeks for the first group, 6 weeks for the second group, and 10 weeks for the third group. Each participant, once per week over the 4 weeks of the program, completed a test anxiety scale 1 hr before an exam and a generalized anxiety scale immediately after an exam. Also, participants completed the test anxiety and generalized anxiety scales 2 months after finishing the program. The researchers presented their results as shown in Figure 4.24.

Variables for Example 4.11

Independent Variable

1. Test anxiety program

Dependent Variables

1. Generalized anxiety scale
2. Test anxiety scale

Figure 4.24.

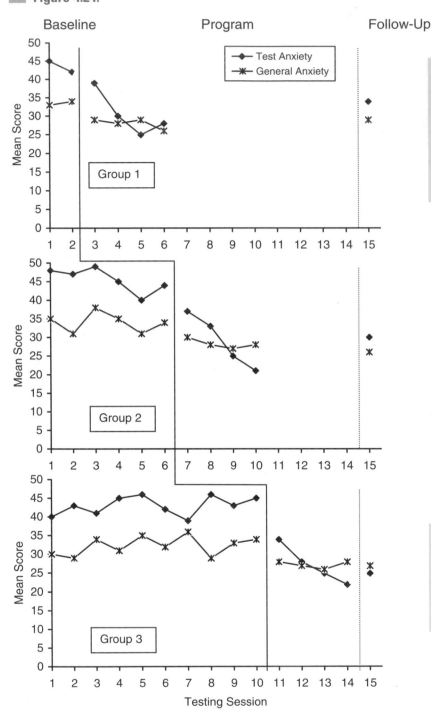

The solid vertical line in this figure divides baseline measures from those taken during the program. A dotted vertical line separates the follow-up measures. Titles denoting the stage of the evaluation are at the top.

To avoid clutter, we used one legend and one *x*-axis title for all the graphs. Also, graph subtitles are enclosed in boxes within the body of the graph.

Figure X. Average scores on test anxiety and general anxiety measures for three groups of participants taking a 4-week test anxiety course. Baseline, program intervention, and 1-month follow-up scores are presented for the three groups (Group 1, *n* = 15; Group 2, *n* = 13; Group 3, *n* = 14). Solid and dotted vertical lines separate the three stages of evaluation.

Example 4.12

A researcher wished to examine neurophysiological differences between bilingual and monolingual people when they listen to words pronounced incorrectly. Twenty individuals who spoke both English and French (*bilinguals*) and 20 individuals who spoke English only (*monolinguals*) participated in the study. Both groups of participants listened to English words that were pronounced correctly and English words that were pronounced incorrectly. Among the data collected were *event-related potentials* (ERPs), an average measure of voltage fluctuation in the brain immediately before and after presentation of a stimulus, measured by electroencephalograph at the midline central scalp site (Cz). Results were presented as shown in Figures 4.25–4.27. (For more information and examples on presenting electrophysiological, radiological, and other biological data, see sections 5.26–5.28 in the sixth edition of the *Publication Manual*.)

Variables for Example 4.12

Independent Variables

1. Language group (bilingual or monolingual)
2. Pronunciation of English words (correct or incorrect)

Dependent Variable

1. ERPs (Cz scalp site)

Figure 4.25.

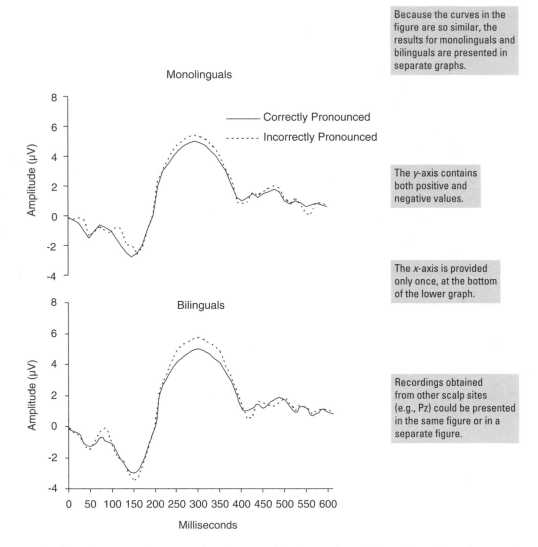

Because the curves in the figure are so similar, the results for monolinguals and bilinguals are presented in separate graphs.

The *y*-axis contains both positive and negative values.

The *x*-axis is provided only once, at the bottom of the lower graph.

Recordings obtained from other scalp sites (e.g., Pz) could be presented in the same figure or in a separate figure.

Figure X. Grand averaged event-related potentials for entire trial as a function of type of participant (monolingual or bilingual) and test word (pronounced correctly or incorrectly). Electroencephalographs were recorded from the Cz scalp site.

Figure 4.26.

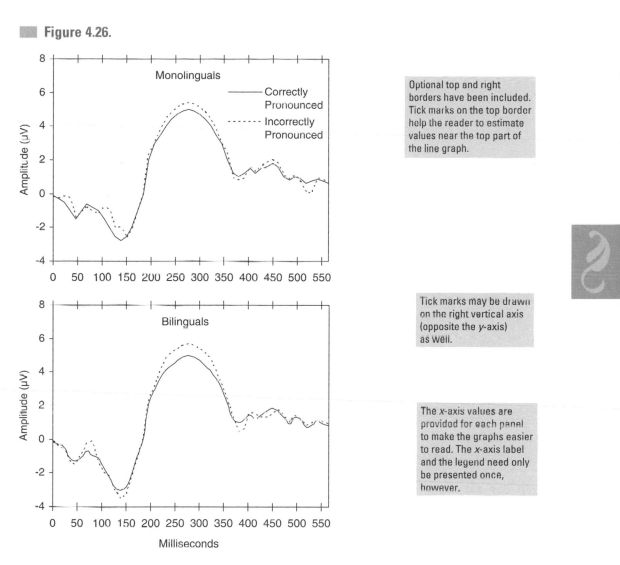

Optional top and right borders have been included. Tick marks on the top border help the reader to estimate values near the top part of the line graph.

Tick marks may be drawn on the right vertical axis (opposite the y-axis) as well.

The x-axis values are provided for each panel to make the graphs easier to read. The x-axis label and the legend need only be presented once, however.

Figure X. Grand averaged event-related potentials for entire trial as a function of type of participant (monolingual or bilingual) and test word (pronounced correctly or incorrectly). Electroencephalographs were recorded from the Cz scalp site.

■ **Figure 4.27.**

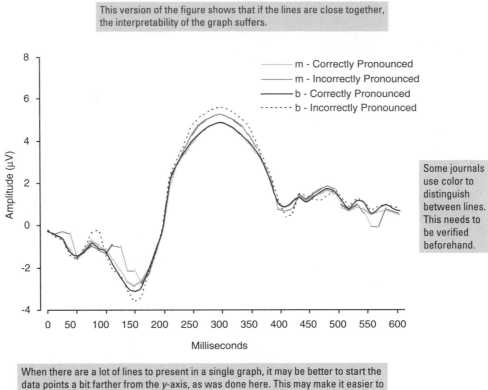

This version of the figure shows that if the lines are close together, the interpretability of the graph suffers.

Some journals use color to distinguish between lines. This needs to be verified beforehand.

When there are a lot of lines to present in a single graph, it may be better to start the data points a bit farther from the *y*-axis, as was done here. This may make it easier to read values for the first data point.

Figure X. Grand averaged event-related potentials for entire trial as a function of type of participant (monolingual or bilingual) and test word (pronounced correctly or incorrectly). Electroencephalographs were recorded from the Cz scalp site. m = monolinguals; b = bilinguals.

Example 4.13

Two researchers wished to examine electrophysiological responses when identifying scrambled words after having named or spelled the word. In the first phase of the study, 20 participants were asked to look at a screen on which words were presented for a brief period. Immediately before the word was presented, a computer voice asked the participant to say the word out loud or to spell it out.

In the second phase of the study, electrophysiological recordings were taken with tin electrodes. The same words were presented as in the first phase, except this time the words were scrambled. ERPs were measured at three scalp sites—Fz (frontal), Cz (central), and Pz (parietal)—and presented as shown in Figure 4.28.

Variables for Example 4.13

Independent Variable

1. Word identification (naming the word, spelling the word)

Dependent Variables

1. ERPs taken at location Fz
2. ERPs taken at location Cz
3. ERPs taken at location Pz

Figure 4.28.

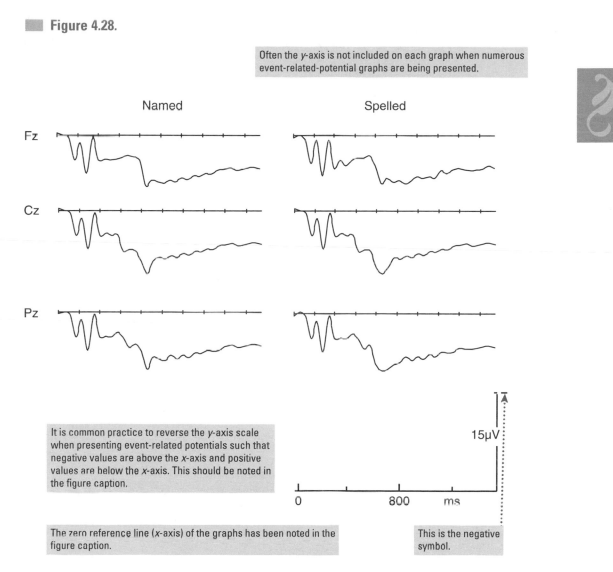

Often the *y*-axis is not included on each graph when numerous event-related-potential graphs are being presented.

It is common practice to reverse the *y*-axis scale when presenting event-related potentials such that negative values are above the *x*-axis and positive values are below the *x*-axis. This should be noted in the figure caption.

The zero reference line (*x*-axis) of the graphs has been noted in the figure caption.

This is the negative symbol.

Figure X. Grand average event related potentials (as measured in Phase 2 of the study) for scrambled words that were named or spelled out in Phase 1 of the study. Electroencephalographs were recorded from the Fz, Cz, and Pz sites. Negativity is up on this figure (the solid line represents 0).

■ Checklist of Effective Elements for Line Graphs

☐ In axis labels and titles, the first letter of the first word and all major words are capitalized.

☐ In legends, the first letter of the first word and all major words are capitalized.

☐ The dependent variable is on the vertical (y) axis.

☐ The independent variable is on the horizontal (x) axis.

☐ The y-axis/x-axis length ratio is appropriate (usually the y-axis should be two thirds to three fourths the length of the x-axis).

☐ Axes are clearly labeled.

☐ Axis labels are parallel to the axes, if possible.

☐ Positive values on the x-axis increase to the right, whereas those on the y-axis increase up.

☐ Negative values on the x-axis increase to the left, whereas those on the y-axis increase down.

☐ There are no more than four lines or curves per graph.

☐ The legend is presented within figure boundaries.

☐ Lines representing the different independent variables within the graph can be clearly differentiated from one another.

☐ Symbols marking data points are the same size as the smallest lowercase letters in the graph.

☐ In multipanel figures (a figure with two or more graphs), the legend and the x-axis title are printed only once if they are identical across all of the graphs. The x-axis title is usually presented on the bottom graph and the legend on the top graph.

Plots

Plots are figures that present individual data points as a function of axis variables. We describe three types of plots: the scatterplot, the group centroids plot, and multidimensional scaling.

Scatterplot

What Type of Data Is Presented?

Scatterplots present values of single events as a function of two variables scaled along the x- and y-axes. The purpose of the plot is usually to explore the relationship between two variables; for instance, a linear relationship may be indicated if the data points are clustered along the diagonal.

Example 5.1

A researcher wished to investigate the relationship between age and vocabulary size. The participants were 70 individuals, 10 from each decade between ages 10 and 80. Participants completed a standardized vocabulary test. Figures 5.1–5.3 present the results.

Variables for Example 5.1

1. Age
2. Vocabulary test scores

■ **Figure 5.1.**

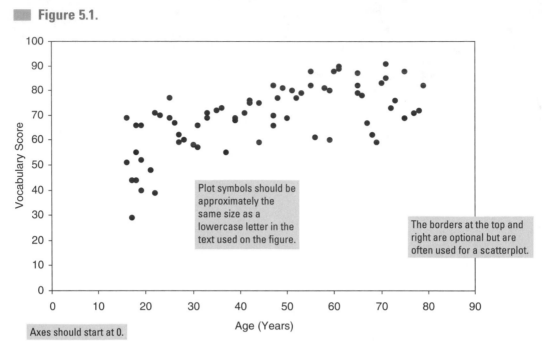

Plot symbols should be approximately the same size as a lowercase letter in the text used on the figure.

The borders at the top and right are optional but are often used for a scatterplot.

Axes should start at 0.

Figure X. Vocabulary scores as a function of participant age.

■ **Figure 5.2.**

The option of presenting the best fitting line and the coefficient of determination is illustrated in this figure.

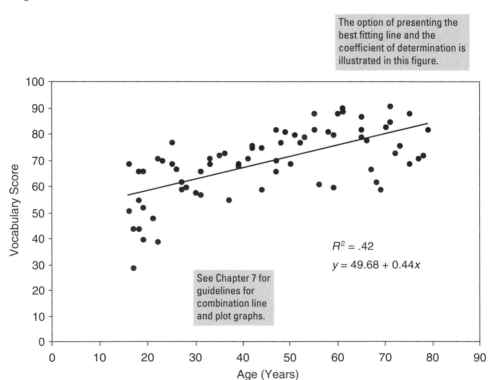

$R^2 = .42$

$y = 49.68 + 0.44x$

See Chapter 7 for guidelines for combination line and plot graphs.

Figure X. Vocabulary scores as a function of participant age.

Figure 5.3.

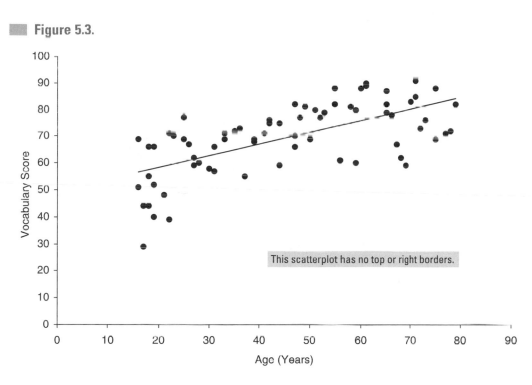

Figure X. Vocabulary scores as a function of participant age.

Example 5.2

The Example 5.1 researcher expanded the previous study to include an investigation of the relationship between age and reading comprehension as well as between age and vocabulary size. The participants were the same 70 individuals, 10 from each decade between ages 10 and 80. Participants completed a standardized reading comprehension test in addition to the standardized vocabulary test. Figure 5.4 presents the findings.

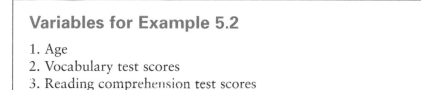

Variables for Example 5.2

1. Age
2. Vocabulary test scores
3. Reading comprehension test scores

Figure 5.4.

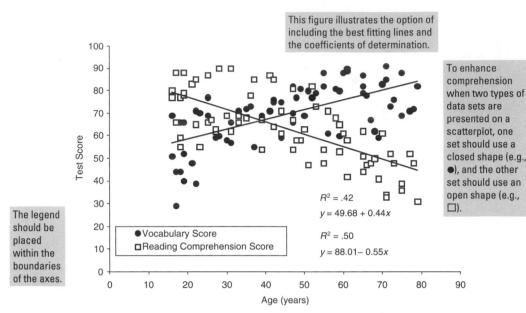

This figure illustrates the option of including the best fitting lines and the coefficients of determination.

To enhance comprehension when two types of data sets are presented on a scatterplot, one set should use a closed shape (e.g., ●), and the other set should use an open shape (e.g., □).

The legend should be placed within the boundaries of the axes.

$R^2 = .42$
$y = 49.68 + 0.44x$

$R^2 = .50$
$y = 88.01 - 0.55x$

● Vocabulary Score
□ Reading Comprehension Score

Figure X. Vocabulary test scores and reading comprehension test scores as a function of participant age.

Although differences between various symbols or lines may be observable on the computer monitor, these differences may not show up once the graph has been printed.

Group Centroids Plot

What Type of Data Is Presented?

Group centroids plots are used to present the results of discriminant function analyses. This type of plot illustrates the extent to which the obtained functions discriminate among groups. Each group in the analysis is represented by a point in the plot. The further away the points are from each other in the plot, the more discriminability has been achieved in the analysis.

Example 5.3

A researcher was interested in the factors that predict the extent to which full-time high school students engage in part-time employment. The researcher surveyed 225 high school students and measured several predictor variables: family income, career goals, level of extracurricular participation, need for achievement, and need for affiliation. The researcher conducted a discriminant function analysis and presented a group centroids plot (Figure 5.5) as part of the written summary of the results.

Variables for Example 5.3

Independent Variables

1. Family income
2. Career goals
3. Level of extracurricular participation
4. Need for achievement
5. Need for affiliation

Dependent Variable

1. Number of hours of part-time employment per week

Figure 5.5.

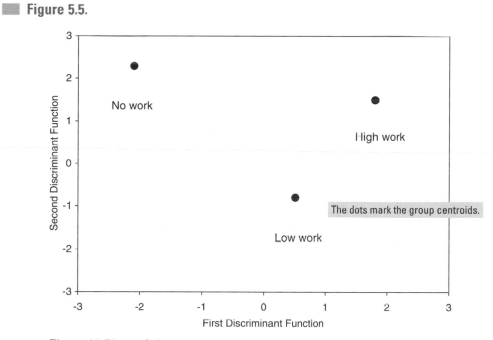

Figure X. Plots of three group centroids on two discriminant functions derived from family income, career goals, level of extracurricular participation, need for achievement, and need for affiliation.

Multidimensional Scaling
What Type of Data Is Presented?

Multidimensional scaling refers to a class of techniques (e.g., individual differences multidimensional scaling, or INDSCAL) that involve presenting similar points or stimuli close together in a multidimensional space and those that are dissimilar far apart.

Example 5.4

A researcher wished to study the perceived cause of maternal feelings in a sample of women with at least one child. The researcher first conducted a pilot study to identify a list of causes for maternal feelings. Once she had a list of causes, she asked a second group of participants to rate how each cause was similar to every other cause. These pairs of causes were presented in random pairs to each participant. Multidimensional scaling was used to analyze the data (see Figures 5.6–5.8).

Variables for Example 5.4

1. Amount of time spent with child
2. Amount of time spent at hospital
3. Age of mother
4. Whether child was breastfed
5. Complications during childbirth
6. Desire to have a child
7. Emotional support
8. Family upbringing
9. Financial support
10. Instinct
11. Knowledge
12. Necessity
13. Personality
14. Role of partner

Figure 5.6.

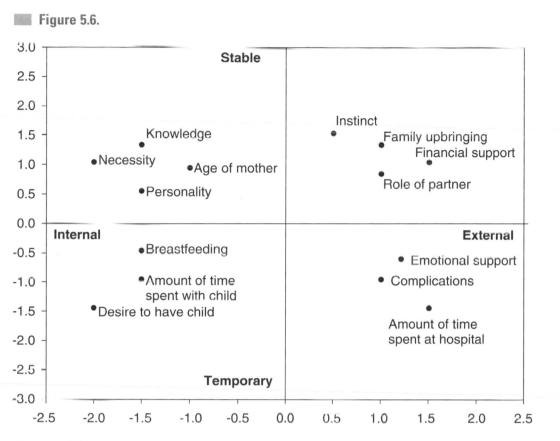

Figure X. Multidimensional analysis of perceived attributions for maternal behavior.

Figure 5.7.

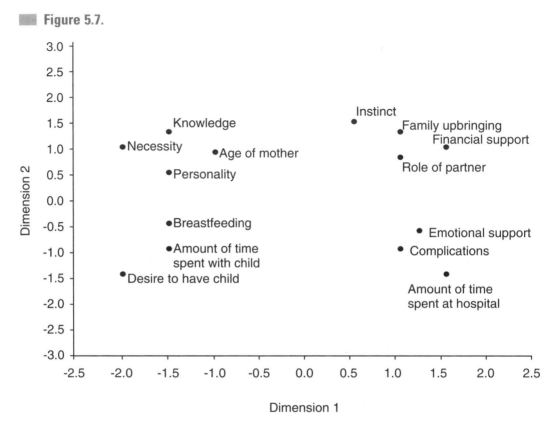

Figure X. Multidimensional analysis of perceived attributions for maternal behavior. Dimension 1 appears to reflect factors internal or external to the person. Dimension 2 appears to reflect temporary or stable factors.

Figure 5.8.

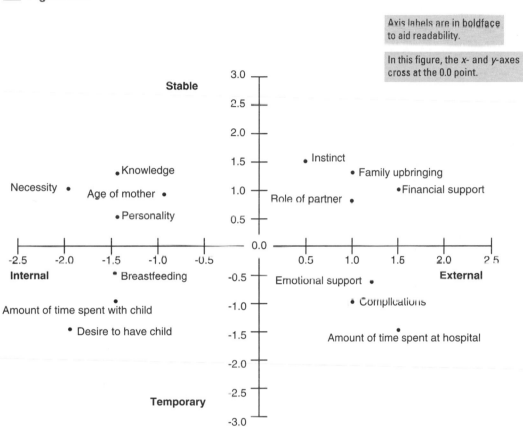

Axis labels are in boldface to aid readability.

In this figure, the *x*- and *y*-axes cross at the 0.0 point.

Figure X. Two-dimensional preference map based on multidimensional scaling analysis of perceived attributions for 14 maternal behaviors.

Example 5.5

Several researchers wished to add to the variables already presented in Example 5.4. In addition to the variables identified in Example 5.4, the researchers included several others that they had found in their studies to be pertinent to maternal feelings. Again, multidimensional scaling was used to analyze the data (see Figures 5.9 and 5.10).

Variables for Example 5.5

1. Amount of time spent with child
2. Amount of time spent at hospital
3. Age of mother
4. Whether child was breastfed
5. Complications during childbirth
6. Desire to have a child
7. Emotional support
8. Family upbringing
9. Financial support
10. Instinct
11. Knowledge
12. Necessity
13. Personality
14. Role of partner
15. Amount of stress experienced by mother
16. Emotional status of mother
17. Level of anxiety experienced by mother

Figure 5.9.

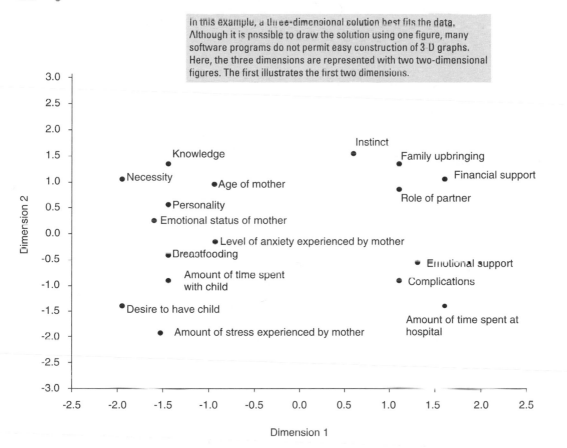

In this example, a three-dimensional solution best fits the data. Although it is possible to draw the solution using one figure, many software programs do not permit easy construction of 3-D graphs. Here, the three dimensions are represented with two two-dimensional figures. The first illustrates the first two dimensions.

Figure X. Multidimensional analysis of perceived attributions for maternal behavior. Dimension 1 appears to reflect influences internal or external to the person. Dimension 2 appears to reflect temporary or stable influences.

Figure 5.10.

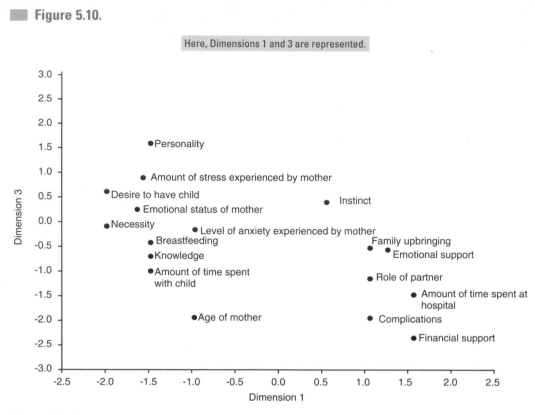

Figure X. Multidimensional analysis of perceived attributions for maternal behavior. Dimension 1 appears to reflect influences internal or external to the person. Dimension 3 appears to reflect emotional versus situational influences.

Checklist of Effective Elements for Plots

☐ In axis labels and titles, the first letter of the first word and all major words are capitalized.

☐ In legends, the first letter of the first word and all major words are capitalized.

☐ Text inside the plot has only the first letter of the first word capitalized.

☐ The *y*-axis/*x*-axis length ratio is appropriate (usually the *y*-axis should be two thirds to three fourths the length of the *x*-axis).

☐ Axes are clearly labeled.

☐ Axis labels are parallel to the axes, if possible.

☐ Zero points are indicated on the axes.

☐ Data points are represented by symbols that are approximately the same size as lowercase letters used in text on the figure.

☐ The legend is presented within figure boundaries.

☐ Regression coefficients and slopes are included for scatterplots if desired.

6

Drawings

Drawings can illustrate a number of different aspects of research. This chapter discusses the presentation of apparatus illustrations, maps, questionnaire items, stimuli illustrations, hand drawings, and handwriting.

Apparatus

What Type of Information Is Presented?

Drawings can be used to illustrate characteristics of the apparatus used in experiments. Sometimes these drawings represent the apparatus alone (Example 6.1), and sometimes they represent the position of a participant in relation to the apparatus (Example 6.2).

Example 6.1

A researcher was interested in the effect of rewards on studying behavior. The researcher devised an apparatus that delivered either a chocolate candy or a quarter (the monetary value of the chocolate candy, 25 cents) each time a participant correctly answered a study question. The researcher recruited 40 college students as participants. All of the students studied a given text and answered questions during the 2-hr experimental session. Half of the participants received a chocolate candy for every correct answer, and the other half received a quarter. The researcher included a drawing of the apparatus in his report (Figures 6.1 and 6.2).

Variables for Example 6.1

Independent Variable

1. Type of reward (candy, quarter)

Dependent Variable

1. Number of correct responses to study questions

Figure 6.1.

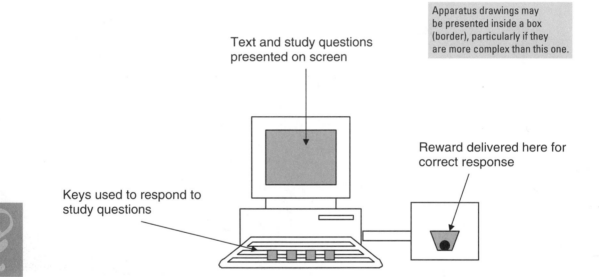

Text and study questions presented on screen

Apparatus drawings may be presented inside a box (border), particularly if they are more complex than this one.

Reward delivered here for correct response

Keys used to respond to study questions

Figure X. Apparatus devised to deliver rewards for correct answers to study questions.

◼ Figure 6.2.

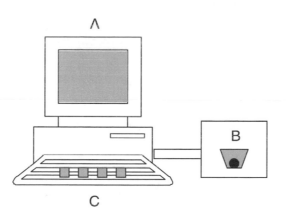

Rather than labels and arrows, this figure uses identifying letters (i.e., A, B, C), which are explained in the caption.

Figure X. Apparatus devised to deliver rewards for correct answers to study questions. A: Text and study questions presented on screen. B: Reward delivered here for correct answers to study questions. C: Keys used to respond to study questions.

Example 6.2

A researcher studied understanding of gravity in a sample of 24 six-month-old infants. The procedure involved dropping a ball behind a screen as the infants watched. The ball either reappeared at the bottom of the screen (as would be expected given an understanding of gravity) or did not reappear (the surprise condition). The researcher measured the infants' *gaze duration*, or how long they looked at the location where the ball should have reappeared. Figure 6.3 is a drawing of the apparatus and participants' locations.

Variables for Example 6.2

Independent Variable

1. Ball action (gravity, surprise)

Dependent Variable

1. Gaze duration in milliseconds

Figure 6.3.

This drawing illustrates both participant position and apparatus.

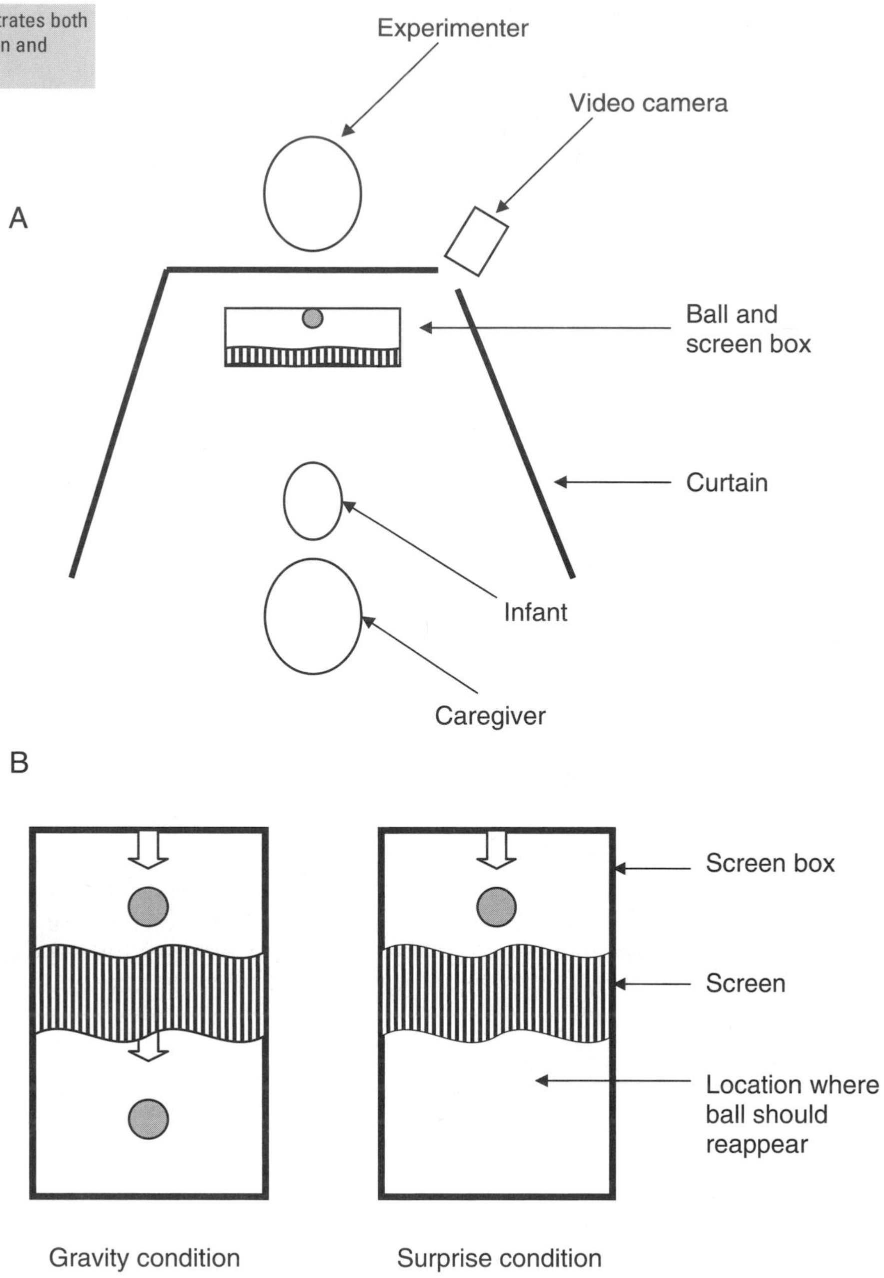

This detail of the screen box could, alternatively, be presented as a separate figure elsewhere in the text.

Figure X. Apparatus used to measure gaze duration. A: Arrangement of infant and experimenter in testing room. B: Detail of ball and screen box for gravity condition (ball reappears when dropped behind screen) and surprise condition (ball does not reappear when dropped behind screen).

Maps

What Type of Information Is Presented?

Maps are used to present spatial data. In psychology, maps are sometimes used to illustrate data as a function of geographic location (but only if geographic location is an important aspect of the study).

Example 6.3

A team of researchers investigated cognitive development in Santay Province, Martat,[1] an area known to have high levels of pesticide runoff in the groundwater. The researchers devised a culturally appropriate test of cognitive development, standardized with 6-year-old children in a nonagricultural neighboring province, and administered it to 6-year-old children in each county of Santay Province. As part of their research summary, the researchers presented a map of Santay Province depicting average number of months of cognitive delay by county (Figures 6.4 and 6.5).

Variable for Example 6.3

1. Cognitive development test scores

▧ Figure 6.4.

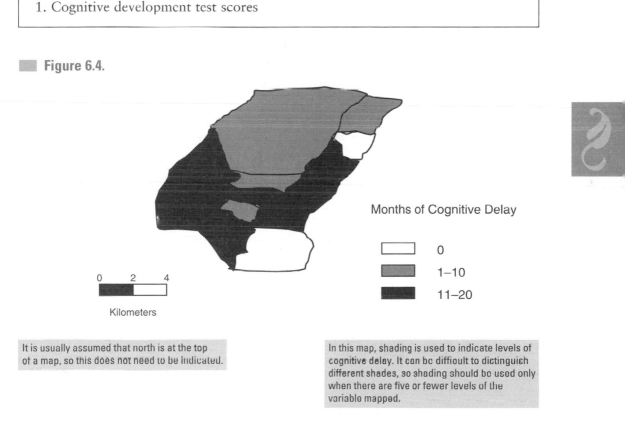

Months of Cognitive Delay

☐ 0
▨ 1–10
■ 11–20

0 2 4
Kilometers

It is usually assumed that north is at the top of a map, so this does not need to be indicated.

In this map, shading is used to indicate levels of cognitive delay. It can be difficult to distinguish different shades, so shading should be used only when there are five or fewer levels of the variable mapped.

Figure X. Map showing average number of months of cognitive delay for samples of 6-year-olds tested in each county in Santay Province, Martat.

---

[1] A fictional country.

■ **Figure 6.5.**

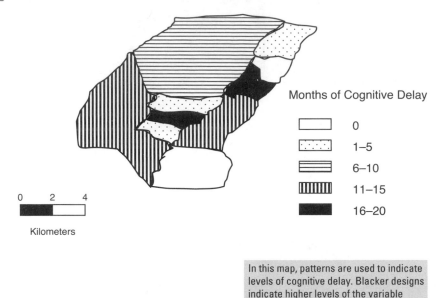

Months of Cognitive Delay

☐	0
☐	1–5
☰	6–10
▥	11–15
■	16–20

In this map, patterns are used to indicate levels of cognitive delay. Blacker designs indicate higher levels of the variable mapped (i.e., cognitive delay).

Figure X. Map showing average number of months of cognitive delay for samples of 6-year-olds tested in each county in Santay Province, Martat.

Example 6.4

The Example 6.3 researchers were also interested in the native languages spoken in Santay Province. They collected information about which languages were spoken in the different regions and presented their findings in a map (Figure 6.6).[2]

Variables for Example 6.4

1. Tali language
2. Lingit language
3. Hon-opa language
4. Stax language

---

[2]All the languages mentioned here are fictional.

Figure 6.6.

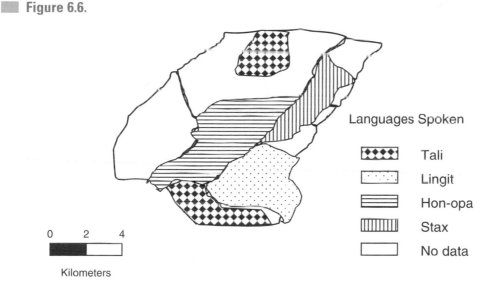

Figure X. Map showing languages spoken in Santay Province, Martat.

Questionnaires

What Type of Information Is Presented?

If a study involves the use of a new or unusual questionnaire, the researcher may choose to present part or all of the questionnaire as a figure. Doing so provides readers with information about the precise format and presentation of the questionnaire.

Example 6.5

Two developmental researchers investigated children's perceptions of sarcastic speech. The researchers were interested in the extent to which children perceived that sarcastic speakers were intending to be mean. The participants were 22 children age 6 years, 22 children age 7 years, and 24 children age 8 years. The children watched six short video segments depicting common events. Half of the video segments ended with a speaker making a sarcastic remark, and half ended with a speaker making a literal remark. The children were then asked to use a 5-point "face scale" to rate how mean they thought the speaker intended to be. In the written summary of this study, the researchers presented the face scale as a figure (see Figure 6.7).

Variables for Example 6.5

Independent Variables

1. Age group (6, 7, 8 years old)
2. Type of remark (sarcastic, literal)

Dependent Variable

1. Face scale ratings

■ Figure 6.7.

NICE   MEAN

Figure X. Face scale presented to children after each video segment.

Stimuli

What Type of Information Is Presented?

Drawings can be used to illustrate the types of stimuli used in experiments. These drawings usually illustrate what the stimuli looked like (Example 6.6). Sometimes, however, it is necessary to represent the way the stimuli were presented across time (Example 6.7) or to depict motion of stimuli (Example 6.8).

Example 6.6

A researcher studying depression was particularly interested in information processing in depressed individuals. In this experiment, the researcher compared performance in picture naming of a group of 25 individuals in treatment for depression with a control group of 25 individuals who had never been depressed. The picture stimuli were line drawings of 40 objects with positive attributes and 40 with negative attributes. The researcher hypothesized that the participants with depression would take longer to name the negative objects than the control participants and that naming times would be equivalent for the two groups for the positive objects. The line drawings of objects were presented on a computer screen one at a time, and participants were asked to name them aloud as quickly and as accurately as they could. Figure 6.8 provides examples of the stimuli.

Variables for Example 6.6

Independent Variables

1. Valence of objects (positive, negative)
2. Depression (depressed, nondepressed)

Dependent Variable

1. Picture-naming latency in milliseconds

Figure 6.8.

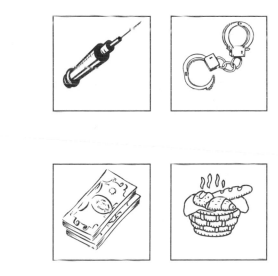

Figure X. Sample line drawings presented in naming task.
A: Negative objects (needle, handcuffs). B: Positive objects
(money, bread).

Example 6.7

A researcher interested in working memory wanted to determine whether working memory was specific to different types of information. For instance, do people have working memory for mathematical information that is somewhat separate from working memory for nonmathematical (e.g., general knowledge) information? To investigate this issue, the researcher devised a dual-task procedure that required participants to draw heavily on their working memory resources (with a primary task) and enabled the researcher to see the effects this had on a separate (secondary) task.

The primary task involved remembering numbers, and the secondary task involved answering questions. The primary task had two levels: Participants remembered either one number (low load) or five numbers (high load). The secondary task also had two conditions: Participants answered either a mathematics question or a general knowledge question. The researcher hypothesized that performance on the mathematics questions would be poorer in the high-load condition than in the low-load condition and that performance on the general knowledge question would be less negatively affected by high load. The researcher's report included a drawing of the trial sequence (see Figures 6.9–6.13).

Variables for Example 6.7

Independent Variables

1. Memory load (low, high)
2. Type of question (mathematics, general knowledge)

Dependent Variable

1. Number of questions answered correctly

Figure 6.9.

Trial sequences can be illustrated in a number of ways;
Figures 6.9–6.13 are some examples.

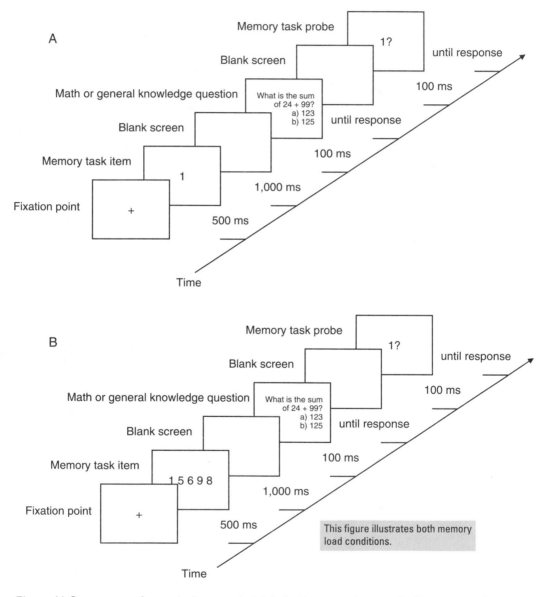

Figure X. Sequence of events in sample trials in the experiment. A: Sequence of events in low-memory load condition. B: Sequence of events in high-memory load condition.

Figure 6.10.

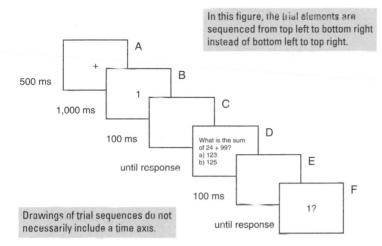

In this figure, the trial elements are sequenced from top left to bottom right instead of bottom left to top right.

A

500 ms

B

+

1,000 ms

1

C

100 ms

D

What is the sum
of 24 + 99?
a) 123
b) 125

until response

E

Drawings of trial sequences do not
necessarily include a time axis.

100 ms

F

1?

until response

Figure X. Time course of events in a low-memory-load trial. In a high-memory-load trial, five digits would be presented at B instead of one. This example trial also involves a mathematics question (at D). For a general knowledge trial, that question would refer to a nonmathematical concept. A: Fixation point. B: Memory task item. C: Blank screen. D: Mathematics or general knowledge question. E: Blank screen. F: Memory task probe.

■ **Figure 6.11.**

This example illustrates the option of combining a table and drawings to present trial sequence information.

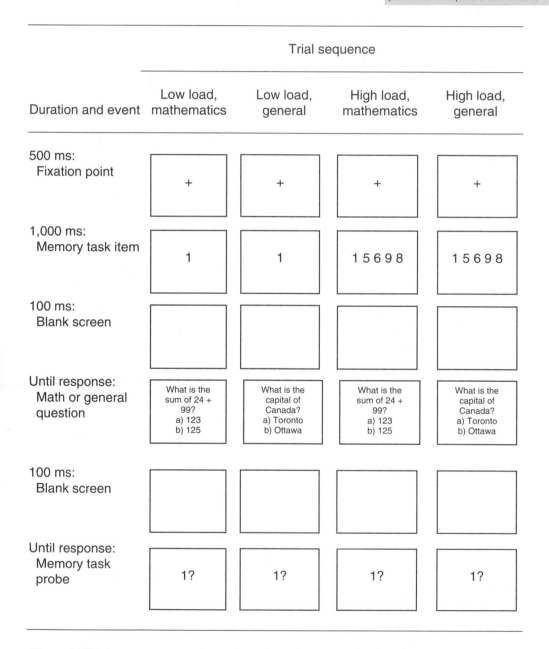

Figure X. Trial sequence used as a function of memory load and question.

Figure 6.12.

This figure presents the trial sequence horizontally, from left to right.

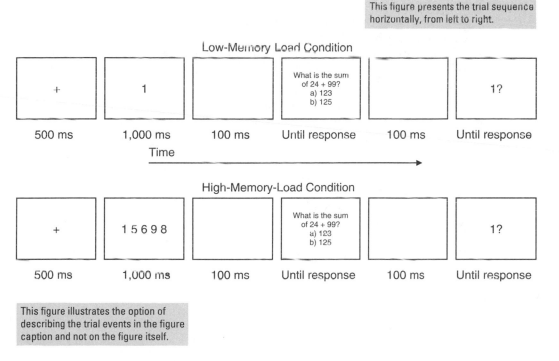

Figure X. Sequence of events during the low-memory-load and high-memory-load trials. Participants fixated on the cross (first panels) and then were presented with the memory task items. After a blank screen, the math (presented in the figure) or general knowledge question was presented until participants responded. After a second blank screen, the memory task probe item was presented, and participants indicated whether they had seen that item at the beginning of that particular trial.

 **Figure 6.13.**

This figure depicts the trial sequence on a time line or axis. This option should be used only when the trial events are quite conventional and have no unusual elements that might require illustration.

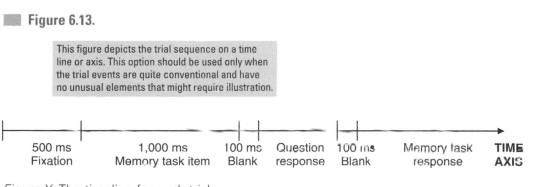

Figure X. The timeline for each trial.

Example 6.8

A researcher investigated how video game playing experience influenced people's ability to track moving objects. The participants, 70 male college students, were asked to report their video game playing habits and were then divided into high-experience and low-experience groups, with 35 students in each. In the experiment, they were presented with target objects (either triangles or squares) on a computer screen. The objects then began to rotate, and the participants were asked to press a button when they thought the target had rotated back to its original orientation. The researcher hypothesized that the high-experience participants would make these judgments faster and more accurately than the low-experience participants. In her report, the researcher included sample illustrations of the stimuli (see Figures 6.14 and 6.15).

Variables for Example 6.8

Independent Variables

1. Video game playing experience (high, low)
2. Type of shape (triangle, square)

Dependent Variables

1. Orientation judgment reaction time
2. Orientation judgment accuracy

Figure 6.14.

> This figure illustrates how motion can be depicted in a drawing.

Triangle Target

Square Target

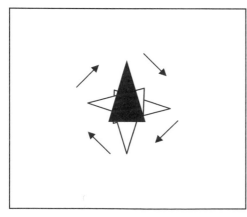 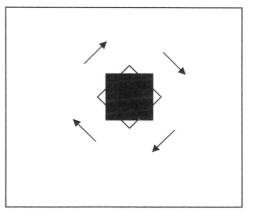

Figure X. The two shape conditions. As illustrated, rotation direction was clockwise.

■ Figure 6.15.

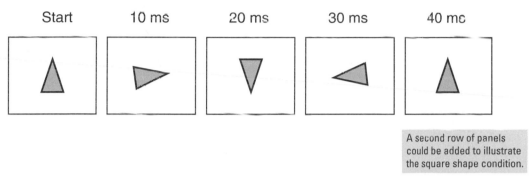

This figure illustrates another way of depicting motion in a drawing. Here, rotation speed is depicted

| Start | 10 ms | 20 ms | 30 ms | 40 ms |

A second row of panels could be added to illustrate the square shape condition.

Figure X. Illustration of rotation speed and direction of rotation for objects in the experiment.

Hand Drawings and Handwriting

What Type of Information Is Presented?

Samples of hand drawings or handwriting can be presented as figures. These might be children's drawings (Example 6.9) or drawings by individuals from special populations. Similarly, handwriting samples might be presented to illustrate the writing of children (Example 6.10) or of individuals from special populations or to show portions of historical documents.

Example 6.9

Researchers interested in how children imagine "scary monsters" asked 20 young children (ages 4 and 5 years) and 20 older children (ages 7 and 8 years) to draw pictures of scary monsters. Each child was given white paper and 12 different colored markers and was asked to draw a picture. The researchers examined the pictures for similarity in terms of three criteria: (a) features, (b) spatial aspects (e.g., size, position on paper), and (c) colors. As part of their written description of the study, the researchers included two sample drawings (with permission; one by a younger child and one by an older child) to illustrate how similar many of the drawings were (Figure 6.16).

Variables for Example 6.9

Independent Variable

1. Age group (4 and 5 years, 7 and 8 years)

Dependent Variables

1. Features of drawing
2. Spatial aspects of drawing
3. Colors in drawing

◼ **Figure 6.16.**

These drawings are presented in frames (boxes) in order to illustrate how the child composed the picture on the pages he or she was given. Often, however, hand drawings are presented without frames.

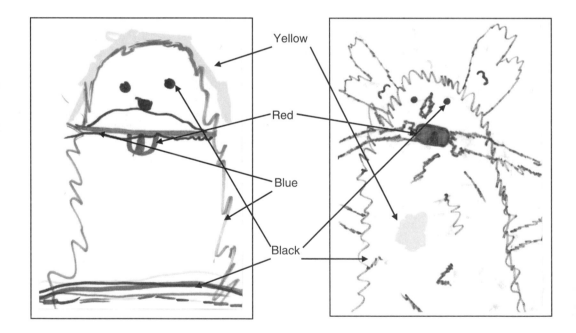

Yellow

Red

Blue

Black

Because pictures are usually published in black and white, it can be helpful to describe the colors used in the drawings. This is particularly relevant in this study example because the researcher included colors used in the drawings as a dependent variable in the study.

Figure X. Drawings of "scary monsters" by a child age 4 years 7 months (left panel) and a child age 7 years 1 month (right panel).

Example 6.10

A graduate student investigating the development of children's writing skills was interested in mirror writing by young children. *Mirror writing* is backward writing, in the sense that words are written from right to left (instead of left to right), usually with each letter facing left instead of right. This type of writing is common among young children, and the researcher was interested in the extent to which early mirror writing (at ages 4 to 5 years) was associated with continued mirror writing and reading difficulties (at age 8 years).

The research conducted was a longitudinal study in which 105 children between the ages of 4 and 5 were asked to produce 20 writing samples. These writing samples were coded for extent of mirror writing. When the children reached their 8th birthday, they were asked to provide 20 writing samples and were tested for level of reading skill (92 children from the original sample of 105 children participated at age 8 years). As part of the written summary of this research, the researcher produced (with permission) a figure showing early and later writing samples for one of the participants (Figure 6.17).

Variables for Example 6.10

1. Extent of mirror writing at ages 4 to 5 years
2. Extent of mirror writing at age 8 years
3. Level of reading skill at age 8 years

Figure 6.17.

For these handwriting samples, the writing is presented without a border (no box around it). If the writing samples involved more words, then boxes around each sample might be an effective way to keep the samples separate.

When presenting two samples for comparison, as in this figure, the scale in each sample should be the same. That is, the samples should be presented so that relative size of the two samples is preserved.

4 years 5 months

8 years 2 months

Figure X. Examples of writing samples produced by one participant. This participant showed mirror writing at age 4 years but not at age 8 years.

■ **Checklist of Effective Elements for Drawings**

☐ Font size is large enough to withstand reduction before printing.

☐ All components of the drawing (especially any uncommon components) are clearly labeled, either on the drawing itself or in the figure caption.

☐ Shading is kept to a minimum and used only when contrast will aid comprehension.

☐ Similar drawings within the same manuscript have a similar appearance.

Combination Graphs

What Type of Data Is Presented?

Combination graphs present two types of graphs within a single figure. For instance, a plot graph may include a regression line, a bar graph may present a line as well, and drawings or photographs may be incorporated within line or bar graphs.

Example 7.1

Researchers wished to study the influence of stress and violence on children's aggressive behavior. They asked 8-year-olds to answer questions regarding their stress level and the amount of violence they watched on television. Each child's parent was asked to rate the child's aggressive behavior. The researchers included a combination line graph and plot graph with their report (Figure 7.1).

Variables for Example 7.1

Independent Variables

1. Stress level
2. Amount of violence watched on television

Dependent Variable

1. Aggression as rated by the parent

■ **Figure 7.1.**

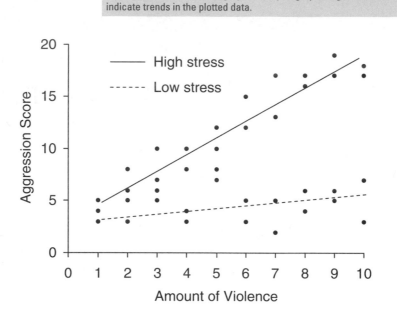

This figure combines a line graph and a plot graph. Regression lines indicate trends in the plotted data.

Figure X. Level of aggressive behavior as rated by parents of 8-year-old children as a function of stress level and amount of violence watched on TV. Computed slopes of regression line for level of violence and stress interaction are presented.

Example 7.2

A researcher wished to determine the ability of a sample of men to correctly match facial expressions. The 2×2 experimental design consisted of two kinds of targets, a male or a female face, and comparison faces that either matched the target facial expression or did not (the target sex was kept constant). Participants sat in front of a computer screen on which the target, followed by the comparison face, was presented. Participants indicated whether the faces matched by pressing a green button if they matched or a red button if they did not. The response times and the error rates of the participants were recorded and presented in a combination graph (see Figures 7.2–7.4).

Variables for Example 7.2

Independent Variables

1. Target face (male, female)
2. Comparison face (similar, dissimilar facial expression)

Dependent Variables

1. Response time
2. Response error rate

Figure 7.2.

Rather than being presented as two separate figures, this combined line and bar graph is presented in a single figure.

The legend has been placed outside the graph because there is no room inside the image area. Legends placed outside the image should be above or below the graph, not to the side.

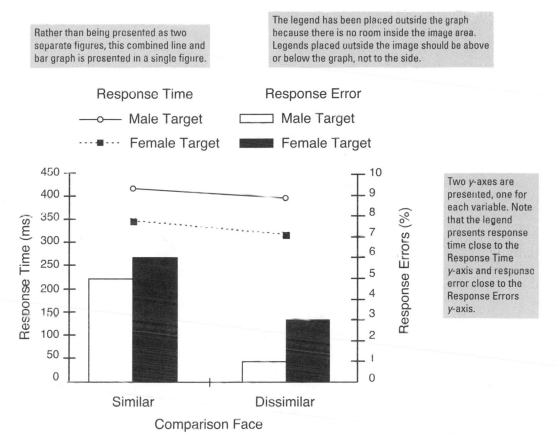

Two *y*-axes are presented, one for each variable. Note that the legend presents response time close to the Response Time *y*-axis and response error close to the Response Errors *y*-axis.

Figure X. Mean response times (lines) and response errors (bars) obtained in the similar and dissimilar comparison conditions of male and female facial expressions.

■ Figure 7.3.

In this example, the % errors *y*-axis extends only a little higher than the maximum error rate obtained rather than spanning the full height of the graph.

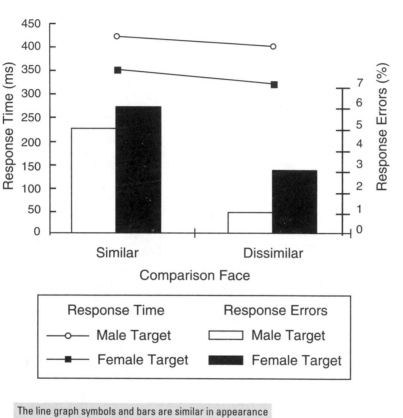

The line graph symbols and bars are similar in appearance (i.e., white for male and black for female).

Figure X. Mean response times (lines) and response errors (bars) obtained in the similar and dissimilar comparison conditions of male and female facial expressions.

Figure 7.4.

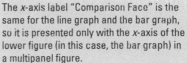

The x-axis label "Comparison Face" is the same for the line graph and the bar graph, so it is presented only with the x-axis of the lower figure (in this case, the bar graph) in a multipanel figure.

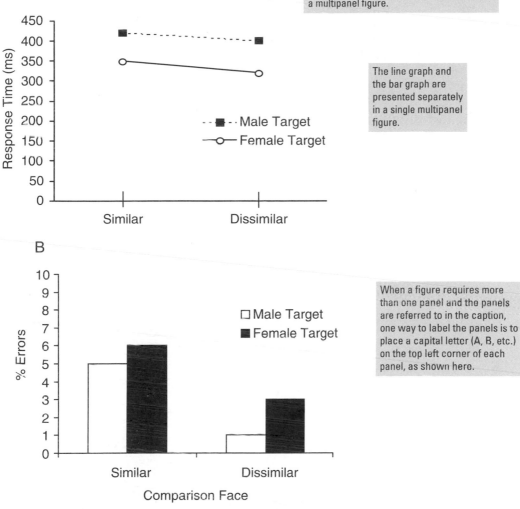

The line graph and the bar graph are presented separately in a single multipanel figure.

When a figure requires more than one panel and the panels are referred to in the caption, one way to label the panels is to place a capital letter (A, B, etc.) on the top left corner of each panel, as shown here.

If panel labels are used, one way to define them in the caption is to follow each letter with a colon and a brief description of the panel, as shown here.

Figure X. A: Mean response time obtained in the similar and dissimilar comparison conditions of male and female facial expressions. B: Mean response errors percentage obtained in the similar and dissimilar comparison conditions of male and female facial expressions.

Example 7.3

Two researchers wished to determine 4-year-old children's reaction times in correctly categorizing shapes. One of four shapes (diamond, parallelogram, square, or triangle) was presented on a screen for 1 s. The child indicated which shape he or she saw by pressing the corresponding shape on a response panel connected to a computer. The shapes were presented on the screen in random order and over several trials. The researchers recorded the response latency and the percentage of correct responses and later used this group as a comparison group in a study of the reaction times of children experiencing mild forms of visual disability. They presented the results in a bar graph that used drawings as x-axis labels, as shown in Figure 7.5.

Variables for Example 7.3

Independent Variable

1. Identification of one of four shapes (diamond, parallelogram, square, triangle)

Dependent Variables

1. Response latency
2. Percentage correct responses

Figure 7.5.

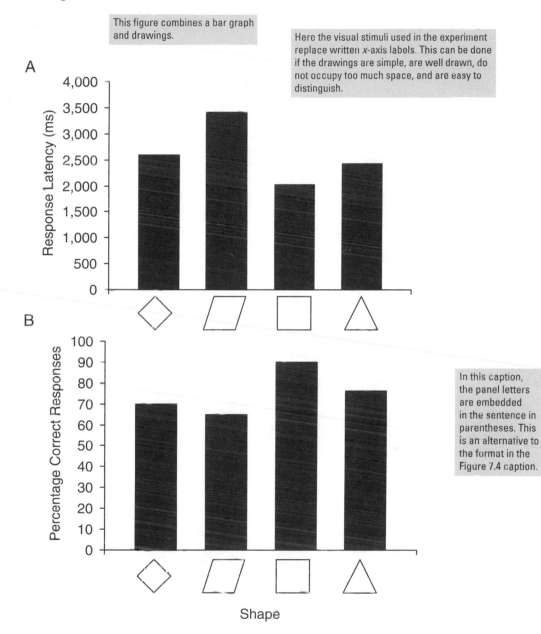

This figure combines a bar graph and drawings.

Here the visual stimuli used in the experiment replace written *x*-axis labels. This can be done if the drawings are simple, are well drawn, do not occupy too much space, and are easy to distinguish.

In this caption, the panel letters are embedded in the sentence in parentheses. This is an alternative to the format in the Figure 7.4 caption.

Figure X. Reaction times (A) and accuracy (B) for identification of diamond, parallelogram, square, and triangle targets in a sample of children age 4 years.

Example 7.4

A researcher conducted a study of teenagers with various disorders and their reaction times in detecting which part of a face was missing. Each of five faces was presented for 500 ms on the screen, and the participant indicated which part (if any) of the face was missing. One face was missing a right eye, one was missing a left eye, one was missing a left ear, one was missing a mouth, and one had nothing missing. The sample included 20 teenagers with attention deficit disorder (ADD), 20 with depression, 20 with obsessive–compulsive disorder (OCD), and 20 without any symptoms of a psychological disorder. The results are shown in Figure 7.6.

Variables for Example 7.4

Independent Variable

1. Type of disorder (ADD, depression, OCD, no symptoms)
2. Identification of the missing part of five faces (nothing missing, no right eye, no left eye, no left ear, no mouth)

Dependent Variable

1. Reaction time to detect which part of a face is missing

Figure 7.6.

This figure incorporates five bar graphs, one for each type of stimuli.

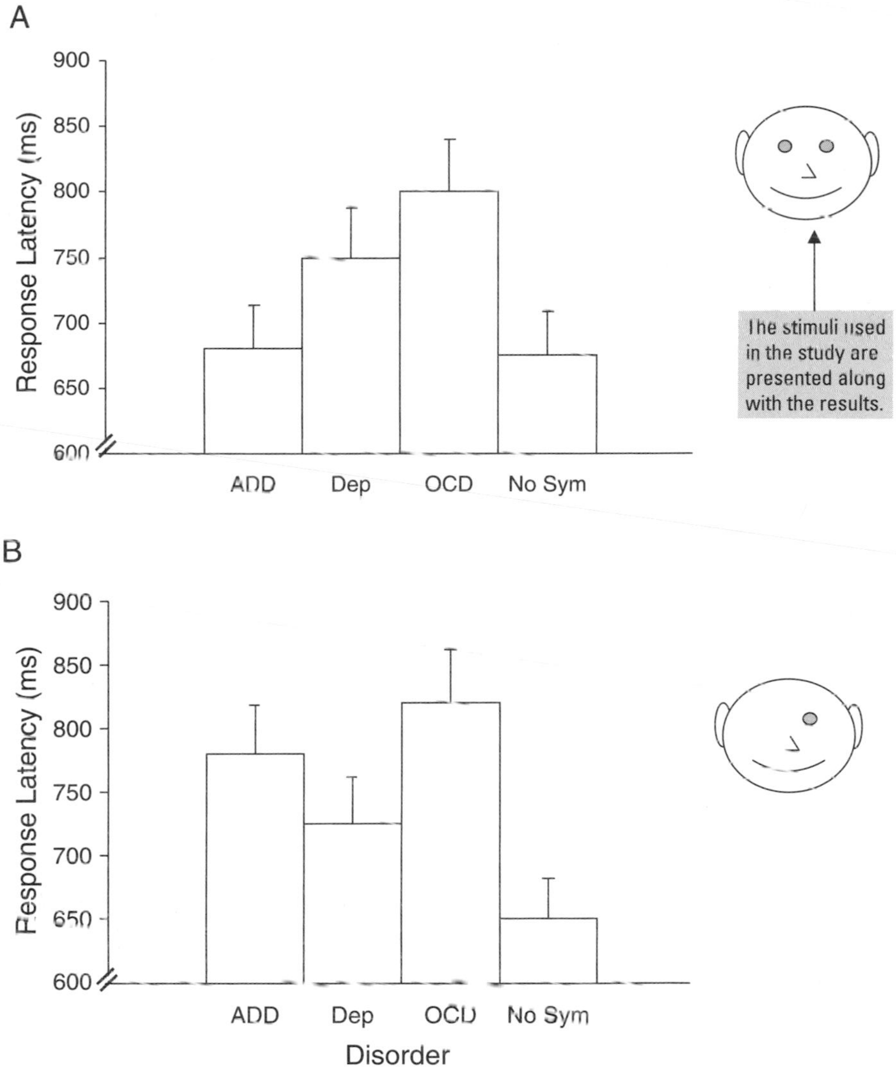
A
Response Latency (ms)
900
850
800
750
700
650
600
ADD
Dep
OCD
No Sym
The stimuli used in the study are presented along with the results.
B
Response Latency (ms)
900
850
800
750
700
650
600
ADD
Dep
OCD
No Sym
Disorder

(Continues)

Figure 7.6. (Continued)

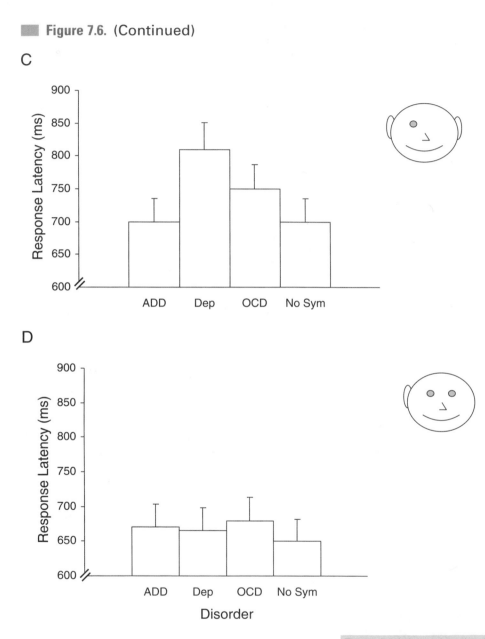

The *x*-axis labels are abbreviated to conserve vertical space. (The full labels are too long to fit horizontally beneath the bars and printing them vertically or diagonally would consume too much space, especially in a multipanel figure like this one.)

Figure 7.6. (Continued)

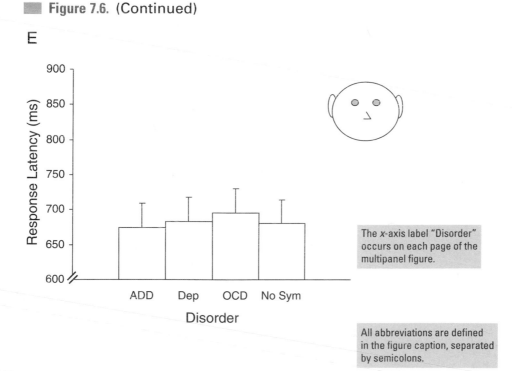

E

The *x*-axis label "Disorder" occurs on each page of the multipanel figure.

All abbreviations are defined in the figure caption, separated by semicolons.

Figure X. Averaged response latencies (and standard error bars) for the four groups of participants as a function of the five different stimuli: nothing missing on the face (A), no right eye (B), no left eye (C), no left ear (D), and no mouth (E). ADD = attention deficit disorder; Dep = depression; OCD = obsessive–compulsive disorder; No Sym = no symptoms.

Example 7.5

Three researchers wished to determine whether a sample of men could distinguish a baby's cry of pain from a cry of hunger. Male parents who had a 6-month-old baby at home were placed alone in a room and asked to fixate on a point. Five-second auditory sounds of a baby crying from pain or from hunger were randomly intermixed and were presented to the participants. Participants had to indicate on a keyboard immediately after hearing each sound which of the two types of sound they thought they heard. As part of their study, the researchers recorded electroencephalographic signals from sites F1, F2, C1, C2, C5, C6, P1, and P2. Average measures of event-related potentials (ERPs) were collected and presented as shown in Figure 7.7.

Variables for Example 7.5

Independent Variable

1. Sound of baby crying (pain or hunger)

Dependent Variables

1. ERPs, F1 location
2. ERPs, F2 location
3. ERPs, C1 location
4. ERPs, C2 location
5. ERPs, C5 location
6. ERPs, C6 location
7. ERPs, P1 location
8. ERPs, P2 location

Figure 7.7.

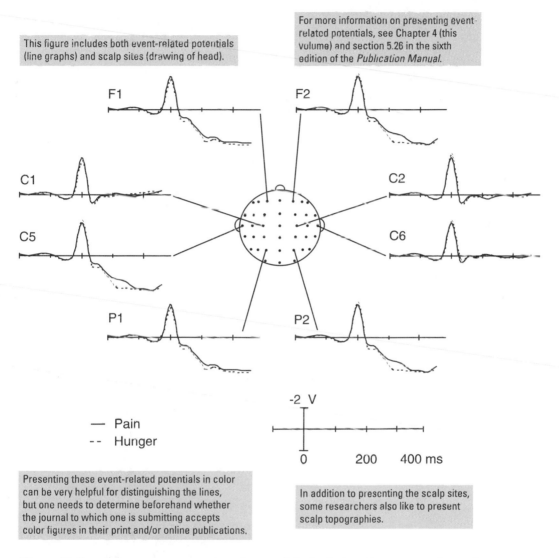

This figure includes both event-related potentials (line graphs) and scalp sites (drawing of head).

For more information on presenting event-related potentials, see Chapter 4 (this volume) and section 5.26 in the sixth edition of the *Publication Manual*.

F1

F2

C1

C2

C5

C6

P1

P2

— Pain
-- Hunger

-2 V

0   200   400 ms

Presenting these event-related potentials in color can be very helpful for distinguishing the lines, but one needs to determine beforehand whether the journal to which one is submitting accepts color figures in their print and/or online publications.

In addition to presenting the scalp sites, some researchers also like to present scalp topographies.

Figure X. Grand average event-related potentials for baby cries expressing pain or hunger in a sample of fathers.

8

Pie Graphs

What Type of Data Is Presented?

Pie graphs (sometimes referred to as *pie charts, cake charts, circle graphs, percentage graphs,* or *100% graphs*) are useful in illustrating percentages and proportions in relation to each other and to the whole. We recommend that no more than five segments be shown in a single pie graph and that the largest segment (sometimes called a *slice, sector,* or *wedge*) start at 12 o'clock, with remaining sections following clockwise. Negative numbers cannot be illustrated in such a graph, and percentages totaling more than 100 should be avoided. In psychology, pie graphs are less common than other types of figures.

Example 8.1

A researcher wished to determine the extent to which the general population read psychology-related literature to seek help. The researcher asked 500 people to indicate the first source they would turn to when they had a psychology-related problem such as marriage trouble, problems with coworkers, lack of motivation, or problems with children. They were asked to select one source from the following choices: academic psychology journals, textbooks, or books; popular psychology magazines; self-help books; advice columns in newspapers or magazines; and psychology Internet sites. The results were presented in a pie graph (Figures 8.1–8.3).

Variables for Example 8.1

1. Consult academic psychology journals, textbooks, or books
2. Consult popular psychology magazines
3. Consult self-help books
4. Consult advice columns found in newspapers or magazines
5. Consult psychology Internet sites

Figure 8.1.

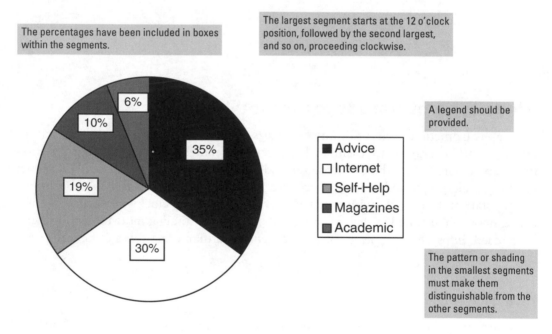

The percentages have been included in boxes within the segments.

The largest segment starts at the 12 o'clock position, followed by the second largest, and so on, proceeding clockwise.

A legend should be provided.

■ Advice
□ Internet
■ Self-Help
■ Magazines
■ Academic

The pattern or shading in the smallest segments must make them distinguishable from the other segments.

Figure X. For five types of psychology-related materials (advice columns; psychology Internet sites; self-help books; psychology magazines; or academic psychology journals, textbooks, or books), the percentage of individuals ($N = 463$) who indicated that the source would be their first choice for self-help.

Figure 8.2.

Color can be used instead of shading for presentation or poster materials to differentiate the segments. Journal or department/university guidelines need to be consulted to determine whether they publish figures with color, whether these are placed online only, and what the file specifications are.

A segment has been displaced from the rest of the circle to highlight it.

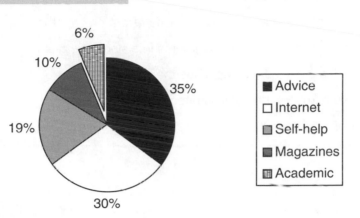

Figure X. For five types of psychology-related materials (advice columns; psychology Internet sites; self-help books; psychology magazines; or academic psychology journals, textbooks, or books), the percentage of individuals (*N* = 463) who indicated that the source would be their first choice for self-help.

Figure 8.3.

Here the legend is eliminated and each pie segment is identified with its label and percentage value.

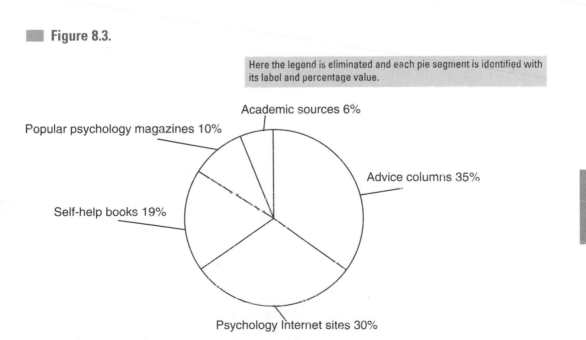

Figure X. For five types of psychology-related materials, the percentage of individuals (*N* = 463) who indicated that the source would be their first choice for self-help.

■ Checklist of Effective Elements for Pie Graphs

☐ Segment labels are all horizontal.

☐ Pie segments can easily be distinguished from one another.

☐ There are no more than five segments in a single pie graph.

☐ A legend is provided that identifies the segments.

☐ Negative numbers are not illustrated.

☐ Percentages total 100.

9

Dendrograms

What Type of Data Is Presented?

A *dendrogram* presents the steps in a cluster analysis solution by illustrating which variables are combined to form clusters. *Cluster analysis* consists of a set of techniques used to identify the structure or grouping of a set of entities. Combined variables are connected using vertical lines. The dendrogram also presents the values of the distance coefficients for each step or vertical line.

Example 9.1

Two honors students wished to create a measure of goofiness. They devised 10 items and decided to first test their measure on a sample of 150 students. They wished to determine the structure of their measure by conducting an agglomerative cluster analysis. As part of their results, they presented a dendrogram (see Figure 9.1).

Variables for Example 9.1

Measure of goofiness:
1. Says silly things
2. Makes funny facial expressions
3. Cannot be serious for long
4. Frequently jokes
5. Has short attention span
6. Selects inappropriate conversation topics
7. Uses frequent hand gestures
8. Wants to be center of attention
9. Frequently laughs
10. Makes verbal noises (sound effects)

Figure 9.1.

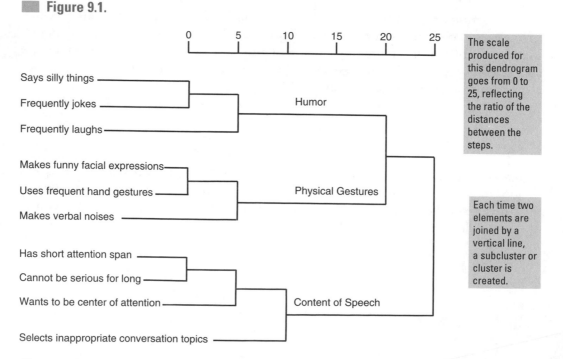

The scale produced for this dendrogram goes from 0 to 25, reflecting the ratio of the distances between the steps.

Each time two elements are joined by a vertical line, a subcluster or cluster is created.

Figure X. Dendrogram for the Goofiness scale based on the results of an agglomerative cluster analysis.

▊ Checklist of Effective Elements for Dendrograms

☐ Dendrograms read from left to right and top to bottom.

☐ The first letter of each word in a cluster is capitalized.

Stem-and-Leaf Plots

What Type of Data Is Presented?

Stem-and-leaf plots present frequencies of raw data while maintaining all of the original data. Each row is referred to as a *stem* and consists, from left to right, of a number (*stem label*), a vertical line, and where appropriate, one or more additional numbers (*leaf*). Each number on a stem to the left of the vertical line is referred to as the *stem label*, and each number to the right of the vertical line is called a *leaf*.

Example 10.1

A researcher interested in the relation between optimism and job performance conducted a meta-analysis to quantitatively determine the magnitude of this relation across numerous published studies. As part of her results, she presented the effect sizes found in the studies she incorporated in her meta-analysis in a stem-and-leaf plot, as shown in Figures 10.1–10.3 and in Table 10.1.

Variables for Example 10.1

1. Optimism
2. Job performance

Figure 10.1.

```
1.7
1.6 | 1
1.5
1.4
1.3 | 3
1.2
1.1 | 9
1.0 | 2
0.9 | 14
0.8
0.7 | 9
0.6 | 0112
0.5 | 567
0.4 | 34
0.3 | 4589
0.2 | 033455789
0.1 | 45
0.0 | 02399
-0.0 | 023448
-0.1 | 23
-0.2 | 3467
-0.3 | 016
-0.4 | 8
-0.5 | 29
-0.6 | 34
-0.7 | 29
-0.8 | 2
-0.9 | 01
-1.0 | 4
-1.1
-1.2 | 2
-1.3
-1.4
-1.5 | 1
 ...
 ...
 ...
-2.3 | 8
```

The stem-and-leaf plot presents all of the raw data in simplified form. For instance, there were zero effect sizes with the values of 1.70 to 1.79, one effect size with the value of 1.33, and one with the value of 0.60, two with the value of 0.61, and one with the value of 0.62.

It is best to place the leaves in increasing or decreasing numerical order. (This figure presents the leaves in increasing numerical order.)

The caption should identify what the numbers in the stem labels and leaves represent.

To save space, three dots take the place of values from −1.6 to −2.2 here; there are no raw data for these stem labels.

Figure X. Stem-and-leaf plot of effect sizes (Cohen's *d*). Stem labels are the ones and tenths places for each effect size. Leaves are the hundredths place for each effect size.

Figure 10.2.

0	1.7	
1	1.6	1
0	1.5	
0	1.4	
1	1.3	3
0	1.2	
1	1.1	9
1	1.0	2
2	0.9	14
0	0.8	
1	0.7	9
4	0.6	0112
3	0.5	567
2	0.4	34
4	0.3	4589
9	0.2	033455789
2	0.1	45
5	0.0	02399
6	−0.0	023448
2	−0.1	23
4	−0.2	3467
3	−0.3	016
1	−0.4	8
2	−0.5	29
2	−0.6	34
2	−0.7	29
1	−0.8	2
2	−0.9	01
1	−1.0	4
0	−1.1	
1	−1.2	2
0	−1.3	
0	−1.4	
1	−1.5	1
0	−1.6	
0	−1.7	
0	−1.8	
0	−1.9	
0	−2.0	
0	−2.1	
0	−2.2	
1	−2.3	8

> This stem-and-leaf plot presents the frequencies to the left of each stem label; this is noted in the figure caption.

Figure X. Stem-and-leaf plot of effect sizes (Cohen's *d*). Stem labels are the ones and tenths places for each effect size. Leaves are the hundredths place for each effect size. Frequencies of each effect size are presented to the left of the stem labels.

■ **Figure 10.3.**

Stem	Leaf
1.7	
1.6	1
1.5	
1.4	
1.3	3
1.2	
1.1	9
1.0	2
0.9	1, 4
0.8	
0.7	9
0.6	0, 1, 1, 2
0.5	5, 6, 7
0.4	3, 4
0.3	4, 5, 8, 9
0.2	0, 3, 3, 4, 5, 5, 7, 8, 9
0.1	4, 5
0.0	0, 2, 3, 9, 9
−0.0	0, 2, 3, 4, 4, 8
−0.1	2, 3
−0.2	3, 4, 6, 7
−0.3	0, 1, 6
−0.4	8
−0.5	2, 9
−0.6	3, 4
−0.7	2, 9
−0.8	2
−0.9	0, 1
−1.0	4
−1.1	
−1.2	2
−1.3	
−1.4	
−1.5	1
−1.6	
−1.7	
−1.8	
−1.9	
−2.0	
−2.1	
−2.2	
−2.3	8

This is still a figure, but the table feature of the software program was used to create it. The line separating the stem and leaf could still be included.

Commas can be used to help in reading the values.

Figure X. Frequencies and stem-and-leaf plot of effect sizes (Cohen's *d*). Stem labels are the ones and tenths places for each effect size. Leaves are the hundredths place for each effect size.

▇ Table 10.1.

Frequencies and Stem-and-Leaf Plot of Effect Sizes (Cohen's d).

Sometimes stem-and-leaf plots are presented in a table format.

Frequencies	Stem	Leaf
1	1.6	1
1	1.3	3
1	1.1	9
1	1.0	2
2	0.9	1, 4
1	0.7	9
4	0.6	0, 1, 1, 2
3	0.5	5, 6, 7
2	0.4	3, 4
4	0.3	4, 5, 8, 9
9	0.2	0, 3, 3, 4, 5, 5, 7, 8, 9
2	0.1	4, 5
5	0.0	0, 2, 3, 9, 9
6	−0.0	0, 2, 3, 4, 4, 8
2	−0.1	2, 3
4	−0.2	3, 4, 6, 7
3	−0.3	0, 1, 6
1	−0.4	8
2	−0.5	2, 9
2	−0.6	3, 4
2	−0.7	2, 9
1	−0.8	2
2	−0.9	0, 1
1	−1.0	4
1	−1.2	2
1	−1.5	1
1	−2.3	8

Note. Stem labels are the ones and tenths places for each effect size. Leaves are the hundredths place for each effect size.

Example 10.2

The researcher interested in the relation between optimism and job performance (described in Example 10.1) also wished to determine whether there were differences in the relation in two populations: blue-collar workers and white-collar workers. A meta-analysis was conducted, and the researcher presented the resulting effect sizes with a stem-and-leaf plot, as shown in Figure 10.4.

Variables for Example 10.2

1. Blue-collar workers versus white-collar workers
2. Optimism
3. Job performance

■ **Figure 10.4.**

Blue-collar workers		White-collar workers
Leaf	Stem	Leaf
1	1.7	
	1.6	
	1.5	
9	1.4	2
4, 5	1.3	1
	1.2	9
1, 1, 2, 6	1.1	8
3, 2	1.0	2, 4, 6
3, 5, 7	0.9	5
4, 4, 6, 6, 8	0.8	7
1, 1, 2, 2, 2, 9, 9	0.7	0
2, 3, 3, 4, 4, 6, 7, 8	0.6	4, 4, 8
4, 5, 7, 8, 8, 8, 9, 9, 9, 9	0.5	2, 9
3, 4, 5, 6	0.4	1, 7
2, 5, 6, 6, 7, 8, 8	0.3	4, 4, 5, 5, 7, 8, 8, 8
1, 2, 3, 4, 4	0.2	1, 2, 2, 2, 6, 7, 9, 9, 9
7, 7, 7, 8, 9	0.1	0, 0, 3, 4, 5, 6, 6, 7, 8, 8, 8
3, 4, 5, 6	0.0	1, 3, 5, 6, 6
1, 2	−0.0	2, 2, 4, 4, 7, 7
	−0.1	2, 5, 7
3, 6	−0.2	0, 4, 4, 8
	−0.3	1, 2
4	−0.4	1, 9
	−0.5	3
	−0.6	4
5	−0.7	5
	−0.8	6, 7
	−0.9	9
	−1.0	1, 3
	−1.1	7
	−1.2	1, 2
	−1.3	3, 2, 1
	−1.4	
	−1.5	4
	−1.6	

To compare across the two populations, we presented the stem-and-leaf plot for both types of workers in the same figure.

Figure X. Frequencies and stem-and-leaf plot of effect sizes (Cohen's *d*). Stem labels are the ones and tenths places for each effect size. Leaves are the hundredths place for each effect size.

■ Checklist of Effective Elements for Stem-and-Leaf Plots

☐ Stems and leaves are clearly identified in the figure caption or in the figure itself.

11

Charts

What Type of Data Is Presented?

Charts are used to present models (e.g., conceptual or theoretical models, structural equation models, confirmatory factor analysis models) and progression through a procedure or system (flowcharts). They are also used to present the results of mediator or moderator analyses, structural equation analyses, and confirmatory factor analyses or the flow of participants in a randomized clinical trial (e.g., Consolidated Standards of Reporting Trials [CONSORT]; see http://www.consort-statement.org/). Charts consist of enclosed boxes, squares, or circles connected with straight or curved lines or arrows.

Example 11.1

A researcher conducted a case study of Company TA's communication lines between employees and their supervisors to identify the different ways individuals communicate with one another according to their level within the company. He created an organizational chart, as shown in Figure 11.1, to provide a visual presentation of the various levels within the organization.

Variables for Example 11.1

Independent Variable

1. Occupation level within an organization

Dependent Variable

1. Communication style

■ **Figure 11.1.**

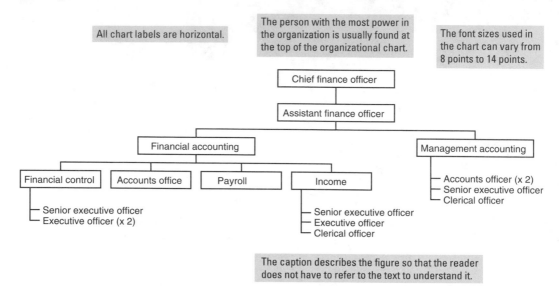

Figure X. Organizational structure of Company TA illustrating the direct lines of communication.

Example 11.2

A researcher designed a conceptual model of determinants of compliance with medication regimens in cancer patients. She supplemented her written description of the theoretical background and the various components of the model with a figure to help readers easily comprehend the model (see Figures 11.2–11.5).

Variables for Example 11.2

1. Individual characteristics (personal variables, demographic variables)
2. Attitudes and beliefs regarding taking medication
3. Commitment to taking medication
4. Situational constraints (number of people living with, available time, support from others)
5. Intention to comply
6. Compliance (frequency of regular usage, number of times medication not taken)

Figure 11.2.

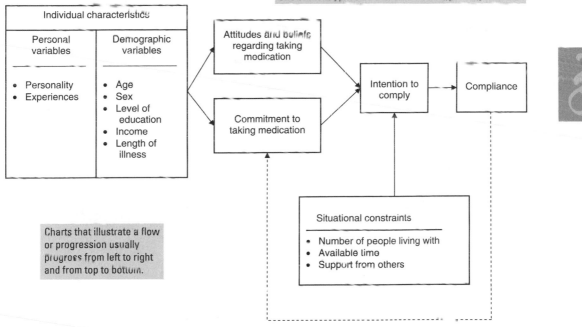

Figure X. Conceptual model of determinants of cancer patients' compliance in taking medication. Dashed arrow indicates the reciprocal nature of the model.

Figure 11.3.

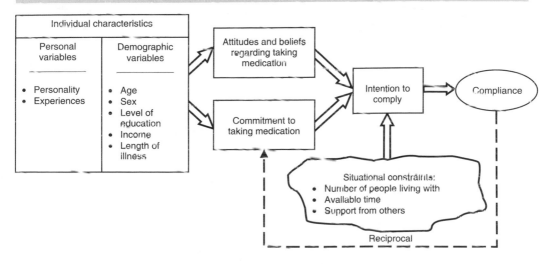

Figure X. Conceptual model of determinants of cancer patients' compliance in taking medication. Boxes represent preprescription measures (measures taken before medication was prescribed), ellipse represents postprescription measure, and irregular shape represents pre- and postprescription measures.

▓ **Figure 11.4.**

Labels are provided over the different variables.

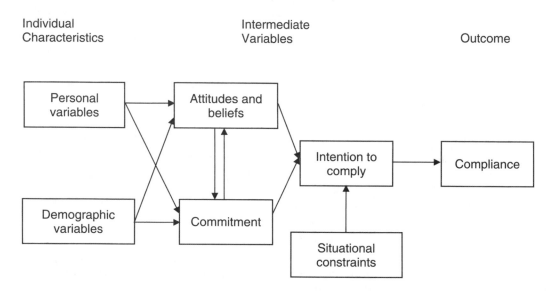

Individual
Characteristics

Intermediate
Variables

Outcome

Figure X. Conceptual model of the three-component model of cancer patients' compliance in taking medication. *Personal variables* include personality and personal experiences; *demographic variables* include age, sex, level of education, income, and length of illness. *Attitudes and beliefs* and *commitment* are those related to taking medication. *Situational constraints* include number of people living with, available time, and support from others. *Intention to comply* is the extent to which an individual intends to take the medication regularly. *Compliance* reflects frequency of regular usage and number of times medication is not taken.

■ **Figure 11.5.**

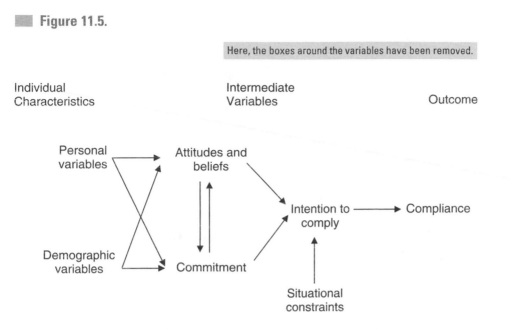

Here, the boxes around the variables have been removed.

Figure X. Conceptual model of the three-component model of cancer patients' compliance in taking medication. *Personal variables* include personality and personal experiences; *demographic variables* include age, sex, level of education, income, and length of illness. *Attitudes and beliefs* and *commitment* are those related to taking medication. *Situational constraints* include number of people living with, available time, and support from others. *Intention to comply* is the extent to which an individual intends to take the medication regularly. *Compliance* reflects frequency of regular usage and number of times medication is not taken.

Example 11.3

A researcher wished to study three aspects of the theoretical model presented in Example 11.2. He wished to determine whether intention to comply is a mediator between attitudes regarding taking medication and frequency of regular usage of medication in cancer patients. He presented the results of the mediator analysis (using regression analyses) as shown in Figure 11.6.

Variables for Example 11.3

Independent Variables

1. Attitudes regarding taking medication
2. Intention to comply

Dependent Variable

1. Compliance (frequency of regular usage of medication)

Figure 11.6.

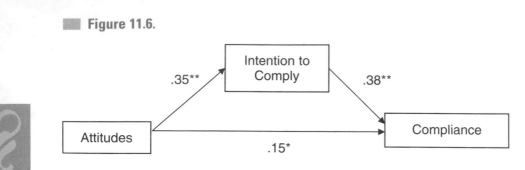

Figure X. Mediating role of intention to comply in explaining the relation between attitudes regarding taking medication and compliance. *$p < .05$. **$p < .001$.

> The *Publication Manual* (see sections 4.35 and 5.16) recommends that exact probability values should be presented if space permits. In charts it is frequently the case that space does not allow this.

Example 11.4

A researcher was preparing a research proposal to study parts of the model presented in Example 11.2. She wished to study the effects of three variables—(a) personality (as measured by conscientiousness and learned resourcefulness), (b) commitment (consisting of affective and continuance commitment), and (c) acceptance of taking medication (as measured by beliefs and attitudes regarding taking medication)—on compliance (frequency of regular usage and number of times medication not taken). She included in her proposal a chart of the causal model she intended to test (Figure 11.7).

Variables for Example 11.4

Latent Variable

1. Personality

Indicator Variables

1. Conscientiousness (x_1)
2. Learned resourcefulness (x_2)

Latent Variable

2. Commitment

Indicator Variables

3. Affective commitment (x_3)
4. Continuance commitment (x_4)

Latent Variable

3. Acceptance of taking medication

Indicator Variables

5. Attitudes regarding taking medication (x_5)
6. Beliefs regarding taking medication (x_6)

Latent Variable

4. Compliance

Indicator Variables

7. Frequency of regular usage (y_1)
8. Number of times medication not taken (y_2)

Figure 11.7.

Charts that illustrate a flow or progression should be presented from left to right and from top to bottom

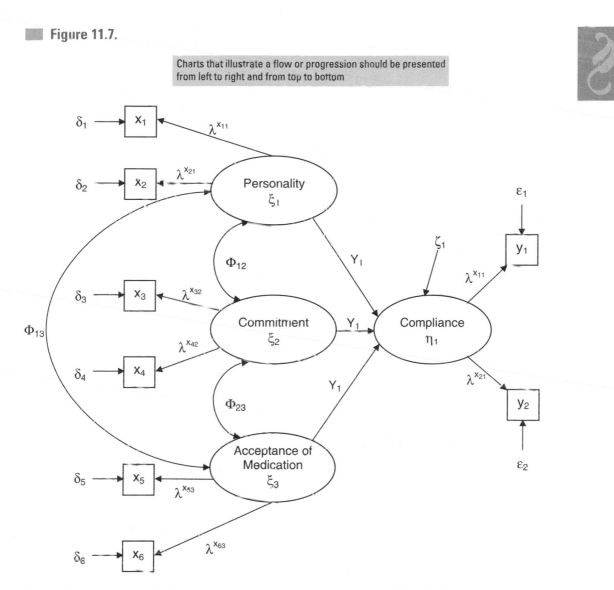

Figure X. Causal model of effects between personal attributes of an individual and compliance. x_1 = conscientiousness; x_2 = learned resourcefulness; x_3 = affective commitment; x_4 = continuance commitment; x_5 = attitudes regarding taking medication; x_6 = beliefs regarding taking medication; y_1 = frequency of regular usage; y_2 = number of times medication not taken.

Example 11.5

A researcher wished to study and test aspects of the theoretical model presented in Example 11.2, in particular the extent to which compliance (frequency of regular usage, number of times medication not taken) is influenced by intentions and whether this relation is moderated by situational constraints (number of people living with, available time, support from others). Furthermore, he believed that several variables may influence a person's intention to comply: personality, commitment to taking medication, and acceptance of taking medication. Personality variables of interest were conscientiousness and learned resourcefulness, commitment consisted of affective and continuance commitment, and acceptance of taking medication consisted of attitudes and beliefs regarding taking medication. The researcher first presented the conceptual model (see Figures 11.8 and 11.9). After conducting the study and structural equation analysis, he presented the standardized coefficients for the model as shown in Figures 11.10–11.13.

Variables for Example 11.5

Latent Variable

1. Personality

Indicator Variables for Personality

1. Conscientiousness
2. Learned resourcefulness

Latent Variable

2. Commitment

Indicator Variables for Commitment

3. Affective commitment
4. Continuance commitment

Latent Variable

3. Acceptance of taking medication

Indicator Variables for Acceptance of Taking Medication

5. Beliefs regarding taking medication
6. Attitudes regarding taking medication

Indicator Variable

7. Measure of intention to comply

Latent Variable

4. Situational constraints

Indicator Variables for Situational Constraints

8. Number of people living with
9. Available time
10. Support from others

Latent Variable

5. Compliance

Indicator Variables for Compliance

11. Frequency of regular usage
12. Number of times medication not taken

Figure 11.8.

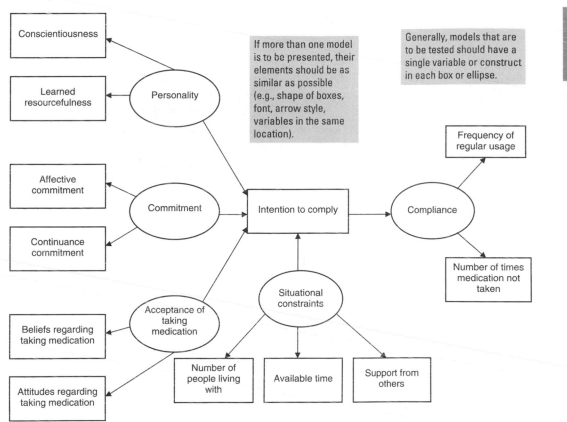

Figure X. Proposed model of cancer patients' compliance in taking medication.

Figure 11.9.

The curved arrow between commitment and acceptance demonstrates a hypothesized correlation between the two latent variables.

The positive or negative relations between the various latent and indicator variables are indicated. (If all of the relations were positive or negative, it would not be necessary to include the symbols in the figure.)

Using symbols can save space. These symbols must be explained in the figure caption in an organized fashion.

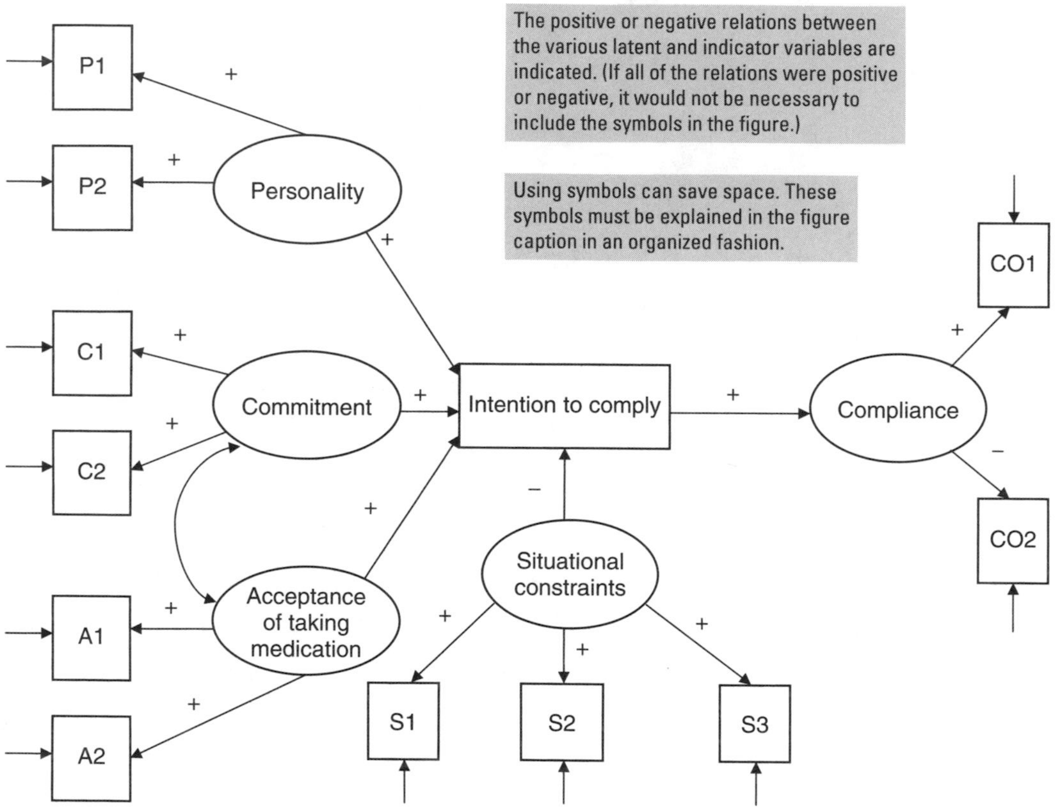

Figure X. Model for cancer patients' compliance in taking medication. P1 = conscientiousness; P2 = learned resourcefulness; C1 = affective commitment; C2 = continuance commitment; A1 = beliefs regarding taking medication; A2 = attitudes regarding taking medication; S1 = number of people living with; S2 = available time; S3 = support from others; CO1 = frequency of regular usage; CO2 = number of times medication not taken. Latent constructs are shown in ellipses, and observed variables are in rectangles.

Figure 11.10.

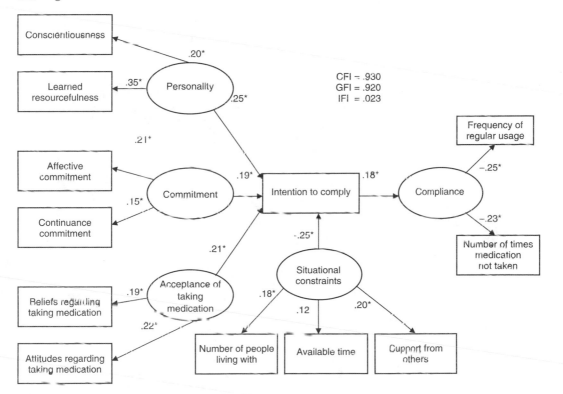

Figure X. Standardized coefficients for final model of cancer patients' compliance in taking medication. CFI = comparative fit index; GFI = goodness-of-fit index; IFI = incremental fit index. Latent constructs are shown in ellipses, and observed variables are in rectangles. *p < .05.

■ **Figure 11.11.**

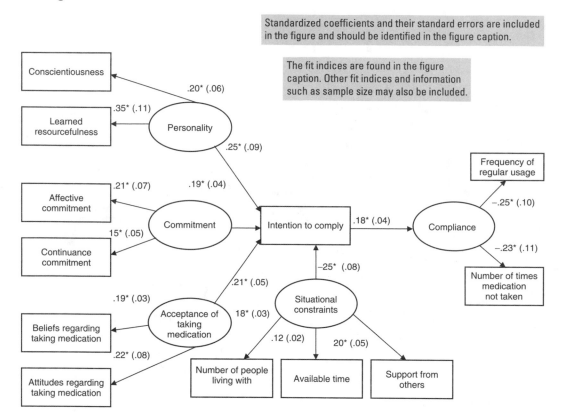

Figure X. Standardized coefficients for model of cancer patients' compliance in taking medication. Standard errors are included in parentheses. Comparative fit index = .93; goodness-of-fit index = .92; incremental fit index = .02; root-mean-square residual = .91. Latent constructs are enclosed in ellipses, and observed variables are enclosed in boxes. *p < .05.

Figure 11.12.

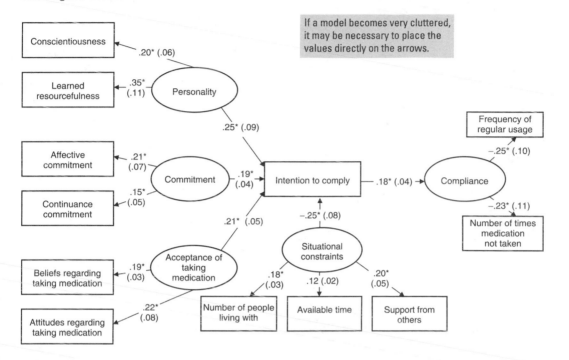

Figure X. Standardized coefficients for model of cancer patients' compliance in taking medication. Standard errors are included in parentheses. Comparative fit index = .93; goodness-of-fit index = .92; incremental fit index = .02; root-mean-square residual = .91. Latent constructs are enclosed in ellipses, and observed variables are enclosed in boxes. *p < .05.

■ **Figure 11.13.**

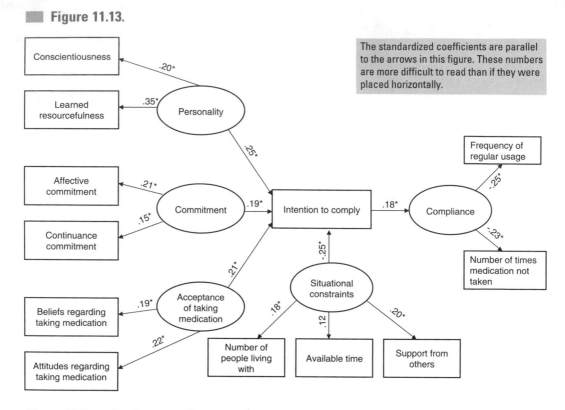

Figure X. Standardized coefficients for model of cancer patients' compliance in taking medication. *$p < .05$.

Example 11.6

Three researchers sought to explore some of the reasons parents place their children in private schools. They developed a decision tree that they believed parents follow when making such a decision. They drew a *flowchart* (a series of lines and text boxes to illustrate the steps involved in a procedure or decision) to depict the various decisions they believed parents make (Figures 11.14 and 11.15).

Variables for Example 11.6

1. Ideology in favor of private schooling
2. Perceived inadequacy of public schooling
3. Close proximity of private school
4. Desire to use alternatives
5. Use of alternatives
6. Adequate financial resources
7. Decision to send children to public or private school

Figure 11.14.

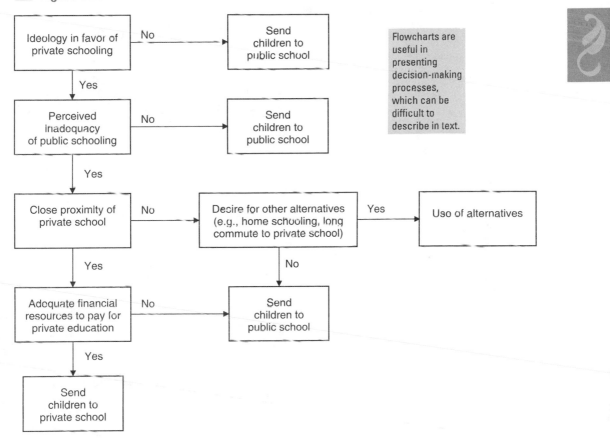

Flowcharts are useful in presenting decision-making processes, which can be difficult to describe in text.

Figure X. Conceptual model of parents' decision-making process when choosing the type of schooling for their children.

■ **Figure 11.15.**

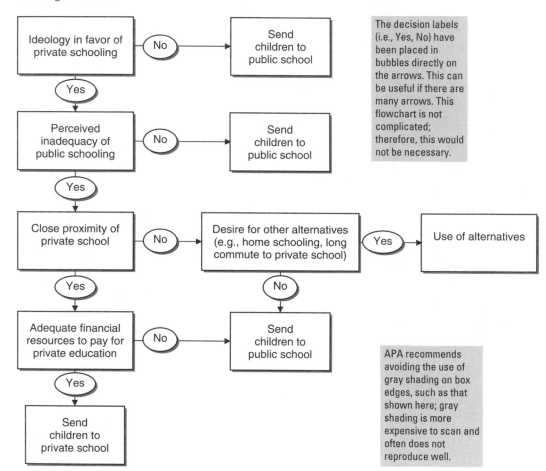

Figure X. Conceptual model of parents' decision-making process when choosing the type of schooling for their children.

Example 11.7

A researcher wished to survey families living in an urban area to determine what percentage of parents living in affluent or poor neighborhoods perceived public schools to be adequate and how many sent their children to private schools. She presented the results of this survey in a figure, shown in Figure 11.16.

Variables for Example 11.7

Independent Variable

1. Neighborhood (affluent, poor)

Dependent Variables

1. Perceived adequacy of public school (good, poor)
2. Child sent to private school (yes, no)

Figure 11.16.

This kind of figure should be read from left to right.

The figure indicates that 81% of the families surveyed lived in affluent neighborhoods. Of those who lived in affluent neighborhoods, 72% believed that the public education system was good, and 28% believed that it was poor.

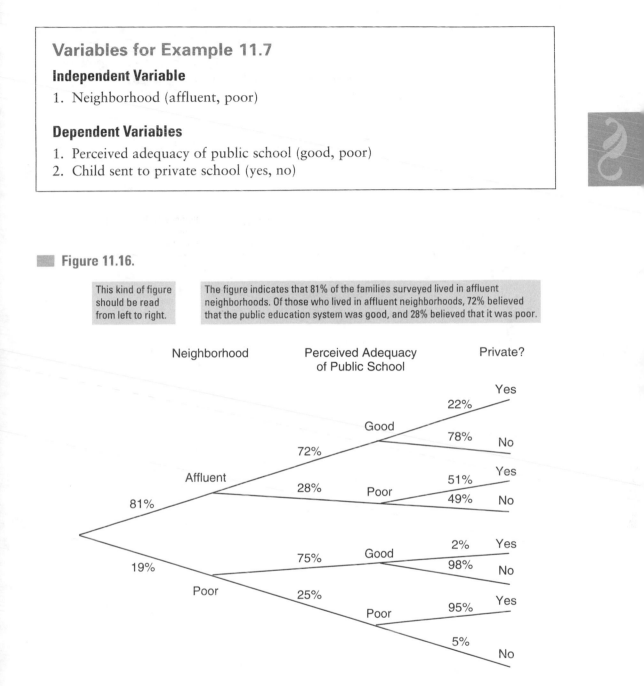

Figure X. Percentage of parents (*N* = 841) who sent their children to private school as a function of their perceptions of the quality of public education and the type of neighborhood they lived in.

Example 11.8

A team of researchers wanted to submit a manuscript to a journal detailing the results of clinical trials of a new drug for multiple sclerosis. Because their research involved randomized clinical trials, the journal required that the team of researchers also follow the CONSORT guidelines. They were required to answer questions regarding the design in a table (not presented here, but an example can be found on the CONSORT website at http://www.consort-statement.org/) and present a figure illustrating the flow of participants in their study. Figure 11.17 presents the generic version of this flowchart published in the *Publication Manual*.

■ Figure 11.17.

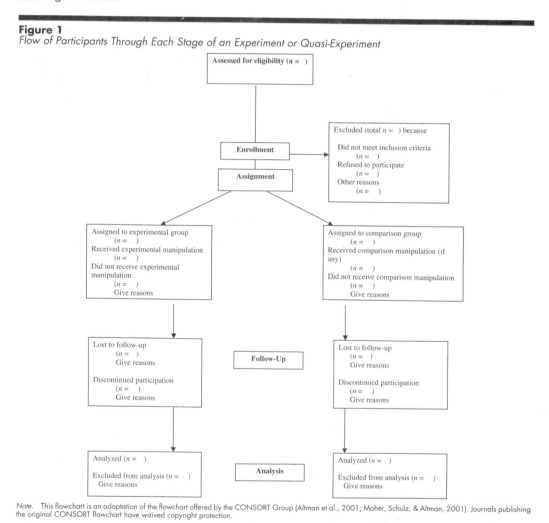

Figure 1
Flow of Participants Through Each Stage of an Experiment or Quasi-Experiment

Note. This flowchart is an adaptation of the flowchart offered by the CONSORT Group (Altman et al., 2001; Moher, Schulz, & Altman, 2001). Journals publishing the original CONSORT flowchart have waived copyright protection.

From *Publication Manual of the American Psychological Association* (6th ed., p. 253), 2010, Washington, DC: American Psychological Association. Copyright 2010 by the American Psychological Association.

Many journals require that researchers follow the CONSORT guidelines as a condition of publication. In some journals, this information is registered. The table and the figure are not necessarily published with the article. For more information, please see the Journal Article Reporting Standards (JARS) published in Chapter 2 and the Appendix of the sixth edition of the *Publication Manual.*

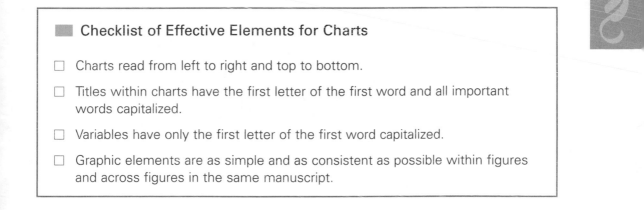

■ **Checklist of Effective Elements for Charts**

☐ Charts read from left to right and top to bottom.

☐ Titles within charts have the first letter of the first word and all important words capitalized.

☐ Variables have only the first letter of the first word capitalized.

☐ Graphic elements are as simple and as consistent as possible within figures and across figures in the same manuscript.

12

Photographs

What Type of Data Is Presented?

Photographs can be used to illustrate procedures or stimuli and to present brain images or slides of tissue slices. Photographs present certain problems. Many journals can publish photographs only in black and white, so the contrast in the photographs must be very strong to be effectively reproduced in print. Some publishers will allow color photographs in the electronic versions of their journals or when photographs include color-specific information relevant to a study (see sections 5.27 and 5.29 in the sixth edition of the *Publication Manual of the American Psychological Association*). In addition, some publishers will print color photographs provided the author covers some or all of the associated costs. Photographs should be used only for illustrations that would be difficult to portray effectively with drawings (e.g., facial expressions, hand positions, and unusual three-dimensional objects).

Example 12.1

Two researchers wished to examine reaching behavior in younger and older adults. They were particularly interested in comparing reaching behavior for these two age groups for familiar and unfamiliar objects. The researchers recruited 30 younger adults (ages 25 to 35 years) and 30 older adults (ages 70 to 80 years). The target objects included six familiar objects and six unfamiliar objects. On each trial in the procedure, participants were asked to reach for and pick up one of the objects. The researchers devised an infrared camera system that measured three aspects of reaching behavior: arm speed, accuracy of arm angle, and grip aperture. The researchers examined how each of these aspects of reaching behavior was affected by age and by object familiarity. In their report the researchers presented photos of sample objects and reaches, as shown in Figure 12.1.

Variables for Example 12.1

Independent Variables

1. Age group (younger, older adults)
2. Object familiarity (familiar, unfamiliar objects)

Dependent Variables

1. Arm speed
2. Accuracy of arm angle
3. Grip aperture

 Figure 12.1.

These photographs illustrate examples of the objects used in the experiment and the type of grasping behavior produced. These aspects of the study would be more difficult to illustrate in drawings.

Elements of side-by-side photographs should be proportional.

Familiar Object   Unfamiliar Object

Color can be used for conference presentations or poster materials (see Chapters 13 and 14 of this volume). However, many books and journals do not print color. Some journals publish in color for articles that appear on the web but not in print.

Figure X. Sample grips used for familiar and unfamiliar objects in the grasping task.

Example 12.2

A researcher studying how meaning information is activated in the brain was interested in whether specific semantic decisions and general semantic decisions activate the same brain areas. Past research implicated the left prefrontal cortex in semantic processing, and the researcher wanted to investigate whether specific semantic processing involves different areas than general semantic processing within the left prefrontal cortex. Participants were 32 right-handed adults. Half of the participants were asked to make specific semantic decisions (e.g., "Is it furniture?") for word targets. The other half of the participants were asked to make general semantic decisions (e.g., "Is it made by humans?") for word targets. In both conditions, participants indicated their responses by pressing a button with their right index finger (for "yes" responses) or their left index finger (for "no" responses). All participants made these decisions while undergoing functional magnetic resonance imaging (fMRI) so that the researcher could measure brain activity. The researcher used brain images to illustrate his findings (Figure 12.2).

Variables for Example 12.2

Independent Variable

1. Specificity of semantic decision (specific, general)

Dependent Variable

1. Brain activity in left prefrontal cortex

■ **Figure 12.2.**

This figure illustrates the option of placing condition labels above the images.

General Semantic Decision

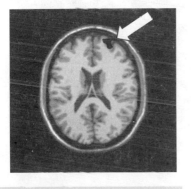

Specific Semantic Decision

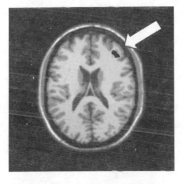

Arrows are used to point to key areas.

The radiographic convention is that brain images are assumed to be viewed from below, with the left hemisphere on the reader's right.

When brain images are presented, the left and right hemispheres should be labeled, either in the figure or in the figure caption.

Figure X. Transverse sections showing activation in the left prefrontal cortex in the two semantic decision conditions. Images are composites for 16 participants each and are displayed in radiographic convention (left hemisphere on right of image).

Example 12.3

A researcher was interested in human memory and the brain areas related to memory. The researcher hypothesized that the hippocampus would be activated by exposure to familiar surroundings but would not be activated by exposure to unfamiliar surroundings. Eighteen participants were shown pictures of their college town (familiar place), and 18 participants were shown pictures of a foreign city (unfamiliar place). All participants were right-handed college students. While participants viewed the pictures on a computer screen, their brain activity was measured with fMRI, and brain images were used to indicate the locations of hippocampal activity (Figure 12.3).

Variables for Example 12.3

Independent Variable

1. Familiarity of pictures (familiar place, unfamiliar place)

Dependent Variable

1. Hippocampal activity

■ **Figure 12.3.**

> Brain images, photomicrographs, and tissue slices are presented in a similar fashion. For photomicrographs, arrows and labels are frequently used to identify particular regions of the images.

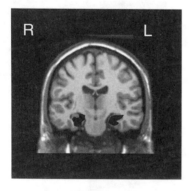
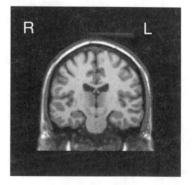

Familiar Place   Unfamiliar Place

Figure X. Illustration of the significant difference in brain activity in the two experimental conditions. Presented are composite images (coronal slice) for 18 participants who viewed scenes from a familiar place and 18 participants who viewed scenes from an unfamiliar place. Darkened areas indicate hippocampal activity. In both conditions there was also activity (not illustrated) in other areas. R = right hemisphere; L = left hemisphere.

■ **Checklist of Effective Elements for Photographs**

☐ The photograph illustrates something that would be difficult to convey with a drawing (e.g., complex 3-D stimuli, faces, body positions, brain imaging results).

☐ Similar photographs within the same manuscript have similar proportions.

☐ Contrast in photograph is strong (for clear reproduction).

13

Posters

A *poster* is a large-format presentation of a research study or theoretical paper. Most conferences have poster sessions, during which authors display posters (usually on large display boards of approximately 4 feet × 6 feet), provide visitors with a verbal description of the poster's main points, and are available for discussion. The aim of a poster is to summarize findings in a clear, interesting way to facilitate comprehension. Ultimately, the aim is for visitors to the poster to understand what the study was about and what the results were. The more visually appealing, well-organized, and informative the poster is, the more likely people are to understand the study and findings.

This chapter focuses on preparation and layout of posters that present research results. Not all posters present research results; posters presenting a theory, a model, or new apparatus, for example, would require different headings and perhaps a slightly different format than the posters described in this chapter.

Poster Preparation

Preparing a poster involves a number of decisions about what information to present and how to present that information. Making a poster involves two (possibly) conflicting goals: (a) to minimize the amount of text on the poster and (b) to make the poster easy to comprehend. To satisfy these goals, some hard decisions have to be made about what—and what not—to include.

Content Decisions

When deciding what information to include in a poster, presenters should ask themselves the following questions:

- What is the main point I want to make? To avoid making the poster overly complex, secondary points should be made only if they are necessary.

- What are the key pieces of information people need to understand my hypotheses or arguments (e.g., previous studies, theoretical models, terms to define)? The answer to this question will decide what is presented in the first sections of the poster.

- Are there any crucial details of my methodology that need to be mentioned? This decision will be influenced by how conventional the methods are. If participants and procedures are typical (e.g., college undergraduates, questionnaire study), then little poster space is required for explaining them. If they are unusual, then a more lengthy explanation may be needed.

- Are there aspects of my methodology that should be illustrated with examples? It may be useful to provide examples of stimuli, questions asked of participants, rating scales used, and so forth.

- Which of my results are the most important to present? Because poster space is limited, a few key findings should be chosen to present on the poster. If a visitor is really interested in the specifics of the data, he or she can discuss it with the presenter or follow up after the conference in more detail.

- What conclusions can I realistically make? A poster presentation is not the place to speculate about the implications of research findings. Conclusions should be limited to those that are strongly supported by the data.

Style Decisions

To ensure the most efficient use of the limited poster space, presenters should ask themselves the following questions:

- How much space will I have? Many display boards provided at conferences allow posters of 4 feet (height) × 6 feet (width), but some are smaller and some are larger. The conference organizers should provide information about the dimensions.

- For every piece of information I have decided to include in the poster, can I find a way to illustrate it (with a figure) rather than describe it with text? Figures are preferable because they attract attention and often save space.

- Will my poster be printed on a series of small panels (*multiple-panel* format) or on one large panel (*single-panel* format)? With computer presentation software and access to a large-format printer, it is possible to print posters on one large sheet of paper. The single-sheet or single-panel poster can be mounted easily at the conference; multiple panels have to be carefully aligned and pinned up. The disadvantages of the single-panel paper can be the cost of printing (although this varies) and the awkwardness of traveling to the conference with a poster tube (needed to protect the large poster).

Poster Layout

Conference posters have a standard layout, illustrated in Figure 13.1. Although some conferences have specific guidelines about poster content (check with conference organizers to determine whether this is the case), conference posters typically have a set of standard components that resemble the sections of a research article described in Chapter 2 of

 Figure 13.1. Standard Conference Poster Layout

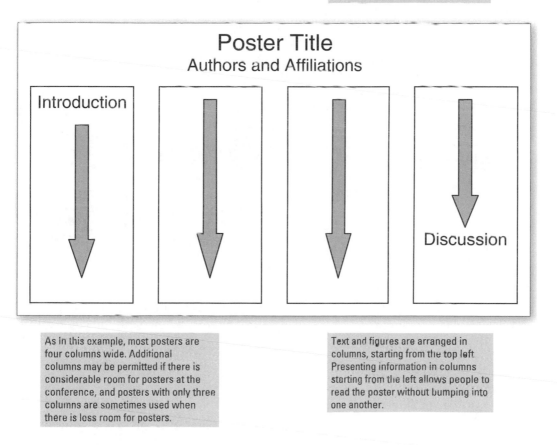

The poster title and authors' names and affiliations are presented across the top of the poster.

Poster Title
Authors and Affiliations

Introduction

Discussion

As in this example, most posters are four columns wide. Additional columns may be permitted if there is considerable room for posters at the conference, and posters with only three columns are sometimes used when there is less room for posters.

Text and figures are arranged in columns, starting from the top left Presenting information in columns starting from the left allows people to read the poster without bumping into one another.

the sixth edition of the *Publication Manual of the American Psychological Association.* Standard poster components include the following:

- title (with authors' names and affiliations),
- introduction (with background information, research questions, or hypotheses),
- Method (repeated for multiple experiments),
- Results (repeated for multiple experiments), and
- Discussion.

Optional poster components include the following:

- university crest (usually placed beside the authors' names),
- abstract (optional; generally printed in the conference program),
- references (optional; these occupy a lot of space and could be provided in a handout), and
- acknowledgments (e.g., research assistants, funding agencies; consider including logos for funding agencies or research centers you wish to acknowledge for supporting the research).

Other Considerations

Besides the questions of content, design, and format, other details need to be considered in creating an effective poster presentation. These include font style and size, use of color, numbering of sections, and creation of handouts.

Font style and size. Many visitors to a poster will be viewing it from several feet away. Thus, the font needs to be large and easy to read. Many veteran poster presenters recommend a sans-serif font for the text (e.g., Arial or Helvetica) and at least 20-point type for text and 48-point type for the title, shown here:

Color. On a poster, the use of color can be very effective in catching the viewer's eye and illustrating results. The following are guidelines for using color in posters. (Chapter 14 of this volume, on presentations, provides information about colors and color combinations that are effective for color-blind individuals.)

- Choose two to three colors and keep them consistent throughout the poster.
- Use strong, primary colors (i.e., red, blue, and yellow). They provide the best contrast and create the most professional impression.
- Use color to highlight key words (e.g., names of conditions, important concepts) in the text. Otherwise, text should be black.
- Avoid patterned backgrounds. They tend to be distracting. Most posters have a plain background.
- Keep lots of empty (white) space on your poster to enhance the effect of colored sections.

Numbering sections. Some poster presenters number the panels in their poster (e.g., 1, 2, 3, etc.) to help visitors follow the sequencing of the panels. Numbering panels is more likely to be useful if the poster involves multiple individual panels (rather than being in large single-sheet format) or if the poster deviates from the standard left-to-right layout.

Handouts. Some conference organizers require that poster presenters bring a certain number of handouts with them to the poster session. These are small, usually letter-size (8.5 inches × 11 inches) or legal-size (8.5 inches × 14 inches) versions of the poster for visitors to take away with them. To save paper, poster presenters may make double-sided copies of handouts. These handouts should be as similar as possible to the poster—ideally, a reduced version of the actual poster (although the font must be large enough to be readable in the reduced size, so it may need some adjustment). If the poster uses color and the budget permits, the handouts should be printed in color. The handouts should include your contact information (e.g., e-mail address) so that you can be asked questions at a later time.

Even if the presenter is not required to bring handouts, it is a good idea to consider doing this because many visitors prefer to just walk by the posters and take a handout to read at their leisure. If the manuscript on which the poster is based has been accepted for publication, some presenters offer a draft of the entire manuscript.

Instead of (or in addition to) handouts, some presenters post a reprint request list on the poster and ask visitors who would like a copy of the poster to leave their mailing or e-mail address on the list. Many conference attendees bring address labels to the conference specifically for attaching them to reprint lists. Presenters who choose to post a reprint list have an obligation to follow through and actually mail or e-mail out the reprints when they return home.

Poster Presentation

Poster presenters are usually expected to be at their poster for a certain length of time. This period could be the entire length of the poster session if the session is only a couple of hours long, or it could be a specified portion of the poster session if posters are to be on display for a longer period of time. During the poster session, many presenters stand near their poster ready to answer any questions visitors might have but let visitors read through the poster themselves. This is certainly acceptable poster-presenting behavior. As an alternative, many poster presenters opt to prepare a short (3- to 5-min) verbal description of the study; when visitors approach the poster, the presenter asks them if they'd like to be "walked through it." Most will accept the offer and enjoy hearing about the study (rather than reading the poster themselves). The verbal explanation should involve lots of references to the poster (e.g., "Here are the results of Experiment 1, and you can see that . . .").[1]

In addition to the poster, presenters should bring the following to the poster session:

- business cards (to give to visitors at the poster),
- thumbtacks or Velcro (the conference organizers may provide these, but presenters should have their own just in case),
- notebook and pen (to jot down issues raised by visitors, to keep track of promises to send stimuli or related papers, etc.), and
- handouts or a reprint request list.

Example 13.1

A researcher investigating how people's moods are influenced by the misfortunes of others devised a manipulation that involved participants hearing a person (a confederate of the experimenter) describe an unfortunate series of events (the person was ill and then caused a car accident). Half of the participants only heard about the misfortunes

---

[1]For further information about preparing poster presentations, consult the following sources: Briscoe, M. H. (1996). *Preparing scientific illustrations: A guide to better posters, presentations, and publications* (2nd ed.). New York, NY: Springer-Verlag; Gosling, P. J. (1999). *Scientist's guide to poster presentations.* New York, NY: Kluwer Academic.

(they could not see the confederate but could hear him or her). The other half of the participants could both see and hear the confederate describing his or her misfortunes. The researcher hypothesized that participants' moods would be more negatively affected when they could both see and hear the confederate than when they could only hear the confederate. There was also a correlational aspect to the design: The researcher wanted to determine whether the magnitude of the mood effects was related to self-perceived driving skill.

The participants were 80 college students (40 in each exposure condition). The procedure involved a single testing session, with four components: (a) Participants completed Mood Scale 1; (b) participants completed a questionnaire about a number of their skills, although the researcher was interested only in the self-ratings of driving skills; (c) the confederate "victim" arrived at the door and described his or her misfortunes to the experimenter; and (d) participants completed Mood Scale 2. The researcher examined how mood scores changed as a function of exposure to the confederate's misfortunes and also how self-perceived level of driving skill related to the extent of changes in mood. The researcher presented the findings of this study at an academic conference using the single-panel format, illustrated in Figures 13.2–13.9.

Variables for Example 13.1

Independent Variable

1. Misfortune exposure condition (victim visible, victim not visible)

Dependent Variable

1. Reported mood

Additional Variable

1. Self-perceived driving skill

Figure 13.2. Overview of a Single-Panel Poster Layout

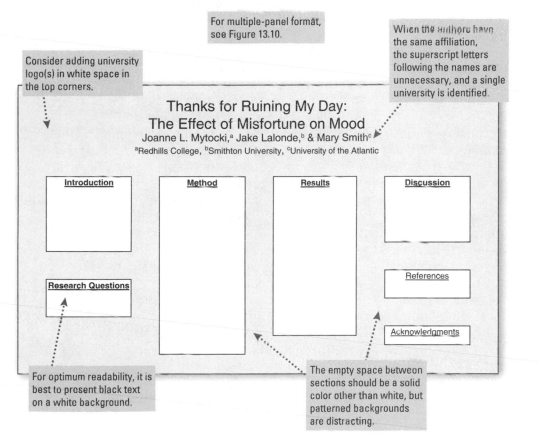

For multiple-panel format, see Figure 13.10.

When the authors have the same affiliation, the superscript letters following the names are unnecessary, and a single university is identified.

Consider adding university logo(s) in white space in the top corners.

Thanks for Ruining My Day: The Effect of Misfortune on Mood
Joanne L. Mytocki,[a] Jake Lalonde,[b] & Mary Smith[c]
[a]Redhills College, [b]Smithton University, [c]University of the Atlantic

Introduction

Method

Results

Discussion

Research Questions

References

Acknowledgments

For optimum readability, it is best to present black text on a white background.

The empty space between sections should be a solid color other than white, but patterned backgrounds are distracting.

Figure 13.3. Introduction Section of Sample Poster

Introduction

Poster text is usually single-spaced.

People's moods are influenced by many factors (e.g., colors, smells, music, tragic events, etc). In experimental psychology, many mood-induction techniques involve exposure to tragic events, such as reading about or viewing a negative situation (e.g., Samuels, 2007; Zeeno & Williams, 2009). This type of mood induction produces a negative mood, presumably as a result of an empathic response. This mood induction technique is typically very effective, and yet there has been little research on the conditions under which an empathic response arises. That is, under what conditions does exposure to another's misfortune have a significant effect on a person's mood? The purpose of the present research was to address this question.

In the present research, one goal was to examine the effect on mood when the victim of misfortune is visible (and not just audible). A second goal was to investigate how feelings of vulnerability relate to mood changes that occur as a result of witnessing another's misfortune.

References are kept to a minimum within the body of the text.

Figure 13.4. Research Questions Section of Sample Poster

Research Questions

1. What is the effect of seeing the victim on changes in mood when witnessing another person's misfortune?

2. What is the relationship of feelings of personal vulnerability to mood changes when witnessing another person's misfortune?

Figure 13.5. Method Section of Sample Poster

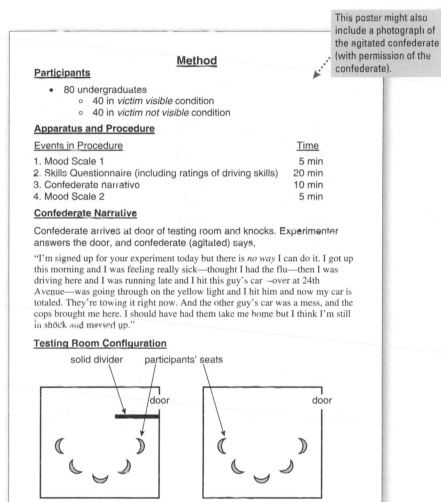

This poster might also include a photograph of the agitated confederate (with permission of the confederate).

Method

Participants

- 80 undergraduates
  - 40 in *victim visible* condition
  - 40 in *victim not visible* condition

Apparatus and Procedure

Events in Procedure	Time
1. Mood Scale 1	5 min
2. Skills Questionnaire (including ratings of driving skills)	20 min
3. Confederate narrative	10 min
4. Mood Scale 2	5 min

Confederate Narrative

Confederate arrives at door of testing room and knocks. Experimenter answers the door, and confederate (agitated) says,

"I'm signed up for your experiment today but there is *no way* I can do it. I got up this morning and I was feeling really sick—thought I had the flu—then I was driving here and I was running late and I hit this guy's car —over at 24th Avenue—was going through on the yellow light and I hit him and now my car is totaled. They're towing it right now. And the other guy's car was a mess, and the cops brought me here. I should have had them take me home but I think I'm still in shock and messed up."

Testing Room Configuration

solid divider   participants' seats

door

door

Victim Not Visible Condition   **Victim Visible Condition**

Figure 13.6. Results Section of Sample Poster

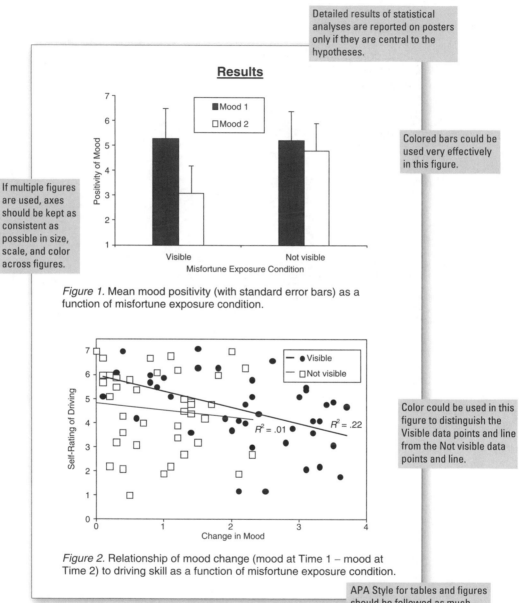

Detailed results of statistical analyses are reported on posters only if they are central to the hypotheses.

Results

Figure 1. Mean mood positivity (with standard error bars) as a function of misfortune exposure condition.

If multiple figures are used, axes should be kept as consistent as possible in size, scale, and color across figures.

Colored bars could be used very effectively in this figure.

Figure 2. Relationship of mood change (mood at Time 1 − mood at Time 2) to driving skill as a function of misfortune exposure condition.

Color could be used in this figure to distinguish the Visible data points and line from the Not visible data points and line.

APA Style for tables and figures should be followed as much as possible.

Figure 13.7. Discussion Section of Sample Poster

Discussion

- Significant mood change only when the victim of misfortune was visible. **Seeing (and not just hearing) someone who has been the victim of misfortune has a significant negative effect on mood.**

- When participants were able to see the victim of misfortune, their change in mood was significantly related to their self-rated driving skill: Participants with lower self-ratings of driving skills tended to have stronger negative mood changes. **Feelings of vulnerability in the context of driving were related to stronger empathic responses.**

- The observed relationship between driving skill and empathetic responses could be caused by the more general factor of low self-esteem (manifested as low self-ratings of driving skills).

Bold text has been used here to highlight general conclusions.

Figure 13.8. References Section of a Sample Poster

The reference list is sometimes left out if space is insufficient. It can be included in the handout.

References

Samuels, K. T. (2007). The effects of mood on creativity. *Journal of the Psychology of Creative Activity, 33,* 18–34.

Zeeno, X. Y., & Williams, J. P. (2009). A bad case of the blues: Color preferences and mood. *Perception and Emotion, 99,* 1–31.

Only two references are presented in this example, but there can be more than two.

Reference lists on posters are often presented in a smaller font than the rest of the poster text.

Figure 13.9. Acknowledgments Section of a Sample Poster

<u>Acknowledgments</u>

This research was supported by a grant from the Generic Research Foundation. The authors thank Greg Smith and Cameron Cox for their assistance with testing participants.

Acknowledgments can be presented in a smaller font than the rest of the poster text.

Acknowledgments can be left out if poster space is scarce. They can be included in the handouts.

Example 13.2

The Example 13.1 researcher presented the results of the study at an academic conference with a multiple-panel poster, illustrated in Figure 13.10. (Note that it is not acceptable practice to present the same study at more than one conference.) The content of individual panels is the same as in the Example 13.1 figures (Figures 13.3–13.9).

Figure 13.10. Overview of a Multiple-Panel Poster

This example illustrates the format for a multiple-panel poster. For single-panel format, see Figure 13.2.

As an alternative, the title could be printed as a banner across several pieces of paper and reconstructed on the poster board.

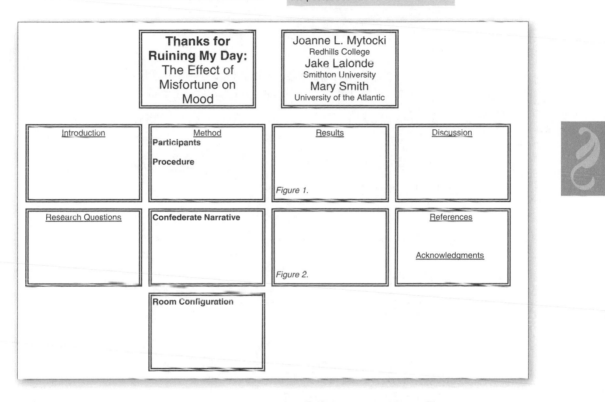

Thanks for Ruining My Day:
The Effect of Misfortune on Mood

Joanne L. Mytocki
Redhills College
Jake Lalonde
Smithton University
Mary Smith
University of the Atlantic

Introduction

Method
Participants

Procedure

Results

Figure 1.

Discussion

Research Questions

Confederate Narrative

Figure 2.

References

Acknowledgments

Room Configuration

Panels can be numbered in the order in which they should be read.

Panels are usually printed on white 8.5-inch × 11-inch paper, in landscape orientation, and often each panel is mounted on a piece of stiffer, colored paper.

Each panel should be limited to 16 lines of text.

▉ Checklist for Effective Posters

☐ Font type and size are consistent across panels (except where a different font is used as deliberate contrast) and across levels of headings.

☐ Text is large enough to be read at a distance.

☐ Text is usually single-spaced.

☐ Only text that is absolutely necessary is included; bulleted or numbered lists and replacement of text with figures and/or tables save space.

☐ Poster sections follow a conventional sequence (e.g., Introduction, Method, Results, Discussion).

☐ Each panel in a multiple-panel poster is limited to 16 lines of text.

☐ The color scheme is consistent.

☐ APA Style for tables and figures as well as text is followed as closely as possible.

☐ If multiple figures are used, axes are consistent in size and in scale across figures.

☐ Only key findings are presented.

14

Visuals for Presentations

A *presentation* is a spoken description of a research study, theory, or model. There are several different types of presentations, including job talks, conference presentations, oral thesis defenses, and guest lectures. This chapter focuses on conference presentations, but many of the guidelines, tips, and examples apply to other types of presentations as well.

Conference presentations are most commonly 10 to 20 min in length, with additional time (5 to 10 min) scheduled for questions. Such presentations are usually grouped in sessions of about four to six related presentations. Conference formats do vary, however, with some involving longer talks by a few selected speakers. Conferences often have parallel sessions (several sessions of talks going on at once). Frequently, conferences include a mix of shorter and longer talks, with some parallel sessions and some keynote addresses that are scheduled alone.

Preparing Visuals for Presentations

Equipment

Computer. Presentation software (e.g., Microsoft PowerPoint) is typically used for conference presentations. This software allows the speaker to design multiple slides for the presentation and to create a seamless presentation that includes text, figures, sound, and video (digital sound and video can be loaded into the presentation file). Graphics can be sophisticated because the software provides a limitless selection of color, sound, and animations.

Presentations on a computer are not without problems. Obviously, they require a computer, which is sometimes provided by conference organizers but often must be brought by the presenter, and also a data projector (i.e., computer projector) to project the presentation from the computer screen to a larger screen. There are a number of ways this technology can fail. For instance, there can be problems connecting the computer to the data projector, problems adjusting the colors created by the data projector, and problems when presentations are created on one platform or with one version of software and then played on a different platform or with a different version of software. These problems can usually be fixed but take up valuable presentation time. It is best to make sure that all aspects of your presentation are working well in advance of your presentation start time by arriving early and testing your presentation.

A word of caution about computer presentations: Sometimes presenters are overzealous in their use of animation (e.g., each line of text "flies" onto the screen from different directions) or sound (e.g., each line of text is accompanied by sound effects). Overuse of animation can be distracting to the audience. The special features of computer presentation software should be used sparingly to enhance key points.

The following tips can help presenters using a computer maximize the effectiveness of their presentation:

- Use sound effects and animation only to enhance a particular point in the talk.
- If possible, use a remote mouse. This will allow you to move away from the computer while speaking.
- Make sure the contrasts between text and background are good under any lighting conditions (a dark room or bright room).
- Practice going back to a particular slide in the presentation sequence. An audience member may ask a question that requires you to show a slide from the middle of the presentation. Also, during the presentation you might accidentally advance the slides and wish to back up.
- Make sure that the presentation is set to advance slides with a mouse click. Presetting a time (duration) for each slide makes the presentation hands free but also requires the presenter to stick to a very strict schedule for the presentation.
- If using a new version of a software program, make sure you also create a separate file for the same presentation and save it as an older version of the program so that if the conference does not have the latest version of the program, you will still be able to open your file.
- Time your presentation so that you know how long it will take.
- Determine beforehand which material you would delete from your presentation if you had less time than you originally thought you would have.
- Practice your presentation with slide transitions.

Laser pointer. A *laser pointer* is a handheld device that casts a small circle of red light onto a screen. Presenters can use it to point to a particular part of a projection screen. Laser pointers must be used with caution; the beam can cause retinal damage if it is cast directly at someone's eye.

Format

Color. The use of color on slides can enhance a presentation. Strong, bright colors should be used, and cluttered backgrounds should be avoided. A consistent color theme should be used throughout the presentation. With the exception of photographs, which can have many colors, no more than two to three colors should be used per slide. The following are effective color combinations that also work for people who are color-blind:

- black on white,
- red on white,
- turquoise on black, and
- magenta on black.

Number of slides in a presentation. Many people find that their talk is well timed if they budget one slide for every 1 to 3 min of talk time. Each should address only one main point or issue.

Fonts. If the slides are projected onto a standard screen, and the room is not too large, a font of at least 24 points should suffice for text (larger is almost always better). The font style and color should be consistent across all slides. Standard capitalization rules should be followed; text in all capital letters is difficult to read. Italic rather than bold or underlining is best to highlight points. A single style for bullet lists should be used throughout the presentation. More than one bullet shape can be used to show different levels of bulleting (as in some of the figures in this chapter), but the system should be consistent throughout.

Text. The text on slides should be as concise as possible. The text should usually take the form of points rather than paragraphs. The text should reinforce, but not match, what the speaker is saying.

In general, slides should include at least the following (not an exhaustive list):

- author's title and affiliation,
- diagram explaining the study design,
- diagram explaining the procedure,
- pictures of stimuli or procedure,
- table or figure summarizing results,
- discussion, and
- acknowledgment of collaborators and funding agencies.[1]

Also, consider preparing an extra slide or two to help answer questions you anticipate from the audience. These might summarize additional analyses or plans for future research designs.

Handouts

Handouts are used in certain disciplines (e.g., linguistics) when the stimuli and examples are complex. When a presenter gives the audience handouts, they can refer back to the examples throughout the talk. Many handouts include only the slides used in the presentation plus any references. Although providing full-scale handouts is an option, a lot less paper is used (and wasted) if more than one slide is included on each page. Handouts can be an asset in talks where the presenter really wants to make a lasting impression (e.g., job

---

[1]For further information about preparing visuals for presentations, consult the following sources: Kosslyn, S. M. (2007). *Clear and to the point: 8 psychological principles for compelling PowerPoint presentations.* New York, NY: Oxford University Press; Morgan, S., & Whitener, B. (2006). *Speaking about science: A manual for creating clear presentations.* New York, NY: Cambridge University Press.

talks) because audience members get something to take away with them and the presenter appears well prepared. The downside to handouts is that the audience can skip ahead, reading the handout and not paying attention to the speaker.

Handouts should include the following:

- a cover sheet with the title of the research, all authors and affiliations, and contact numbers or addresses or both;
- the slides presented as well as any additional images that would not have appeared clearly on a projector;
- efficient use of space—more than one slide is included on each page, with handouts printed double-sided (pages numbered); and
- references cited in the presentation.

Example 14.1

A researcher was interested in autobiographical memory, particularly the nature of the events that are remembered from one's life. The researcher wanted to determine whether people's memory for events is influenced by three factors: (a) age at the time of the memory, (b) how surprising the event was, and (c) how positive the event was. The researcher assessed the frequency of memories for four types of events: surprising positive events (e.g., winning the lottery), surprising negative events (e.g., injury in an accident), unsurprising positive events (e.g., graduating from college), and unsurprising negative events (e.g., death of a parent after a long illness). The participants were 60 individuals aged 50 to 60 years.

Testing involved two separate sessions. The first session was a personal interview in which participants were asked to recount 10 memories from each decade of their lives. In the second session, 2 days later, participants were asked to decide, for each of the memories they had recounted, whether they remembered the event as surprising or not surprising and whether they remembered it as positive or negative. The researcher prepared slides for a 15-min talk, shown in Figures 14.1–14.10.

Variables for Example 14.1

Independent Variables

1. Age at time of memory (decades 0–9, 10–19, 20–29, 30–39, 40–49)
2. Surprise of event (surprising, not surprising)
3. Positivity of event (positive, negative)

Dependent Variable

1. Frequency of memories

Figure 14.1. Slide 1 of Sample Presentation

The Good Old Days?
Investigating the Content of
Autobiographical Memories

Natalie Smith, Jordan Jones, and Kate Green

Anywhere State University

> The text font should be at least 24 points. The color combination should be effective and consistent.

> The first author is usually (but not always) the person giving the talk

Figure 14.2. Slide 2 of Sample Presentation

What Is Autobiographical Memory?

➢ Memory for events in our lives

➢ Changes across life span in the number of memories:

  o Childhood amnesia
  o Reminiscence bump
  o Recency

> Wording slide titles as questions can be an effective presentation strategy.

Figure 14.3. Slide 3 of Sample Presentation

What Is the Content of Autobiographical Memories?

➢ Memories for emotional events (e.g., Cole, 2009)

Unanswered questions . . .

➢ Positive or negative emotions?
➢ Surprising or nonsurprising events?

Figure 14.4. Slide 4 of Sample Presentation

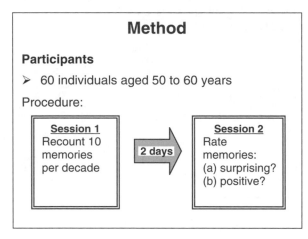

Present Research

Purpose

➢ Investigate content of autobiographical memories
  o Positive/negative
  o Surprising/nonsurprising

Amount of text on the screen should be kept to a minimum.

Figure 14.5. Slide 5 of Sample Presentation

Method

Participants

➢ 60 individuals aged 50 to 60 years

Procedure:

Session 1		Session 2
Recount 10 memories per decade	2 days →	Rate memories: (a) surprising? (b) positive?

Aspects of the methodology are usually presented in the same order they would appear in an APA-formatted paper (e.g., participants, materials, procedure). Font and style will often depend on the overall design requirements of the presentation and may differ from what would be used in a paper.

Figure 14.6. Slide 6 of Sample Presentation

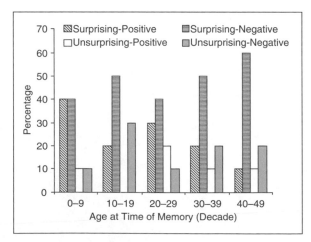

Keep graphics simple.

Figure 14.7. Slide 7 of Sample Presentation

> ## Results
>
> ➤ Proportion of memories for surprising, negative events increased across the life span
>
> ➤ Proportion of memories for surprising, positive events decreased across the life span
>
> ➤ Proportion was higher of surprising than nonsurprising memories across the life span

Figure 14.8. Slide 8 of Sample Presentation

> ## Why More Surprising Memories?
>
> ➤ Surprising = distinctive?
>   - o Many of the memories were of novel experiences
>
> ➤ Surprising = traumatic?
>   - o Many of the memories were of unexpected accidents
>
> ➤ Surprising = life altering?
>   - o Many of the memories were of new and unexpected opportunities

Figure 14.9. Slide 9 of Sample Presentation

> ## Why More Surprising, Negative Memories in Later Decades?
>
> ➤ Erosion of tendency to "remember the good times"?
>
> ➤ Future research required to systematically evaluate these possibilities

Figure 14.10. Slide 10 of Sample Presentation

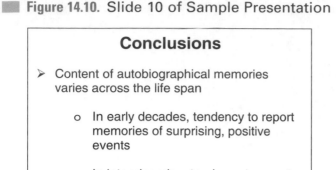

> Content of autobiographical memories varies across the life span
>
> o In early decades, tendency to report memories of surprising, positive events
>
> o In later decades, tendency to report memories of surprising, negative events

A reference slide would require too much text. Presenters can provide references to the audience in a handout.

Checklist for Effective Visuals for Presentations

☐ Font type, size, and color are consistent across slides.

☐ Text is large enough to be read from a distance (at least 24 points).

☐ There are no more than 12 lines of text per slide.

☐ Text is clearly organized (e.g., using bullets or numbering).

☐ Text is limited to that which is absolutely necessary.

☐ One main idea or topic is on each slide.

☐ Color scheme (if any) is consistent.

☐ Color combinations are carefully considered; bright colors give a professional appearance.

☐ If multiple figures are used, axes are consistent across figures where possible.

☐ Only key findings (those related to hypotheses and conclusions) are presented.

Index

V

Values, 72
Variables
    in boxes, 139, 141, 145
    categorical, 59
    dependent, 35, 67
    independent, 43
Velcro, 167
Verbal explanation, of poster, 167
Vertical axis. *See* y-axis
Vertical grid lines, 49
Visuals, for presentations, 177–184
    checklist for, 184
    preparation of, 177–180
    slides as, 180–184

W

Wedge, 121
Whitener, B., 179n1
Wording, 181

X

x-axis
    abbreviated, 116

drawings as labels for, 113
in histograms, 37
labels for, 4, 111, 117
legends for, 68
length of, 16, 43
for multipanel graphs, 73
titles for, 4, 25
values on, 50

Y

y-axis
    break in, 23
    dependent variables on, 16
    duplicate on right, 34
    labels for, 4
    length of, 16, 43, 68
    mean totals on, 21
    more than one, 110
    reversed scale on, 75
    starting point of, 32, 58
    titles for, 4

Z

Zero reference line, 75

About the Authors

Adelheid A. M. Nicol, PhD, received her doctorate in industrial/organizational psychology from the University of Western Ontario, London, Ontario, Canada, in 1999. She is an associate professor in the Military Psychology and Leadership Department at the Royal Military College of Canada, Kingston, Ontario, Canada. Her current research interests are in the area of prejudice and industrial/organizational psychology. She teaches courses in English and in French in cross-cultural psychology, industrial psychology, organizational psychology, personality, research methods, and social psychology.

Penny M. Pexman, PhD, earned her doctorate in psychology from the University of Western Ontario, London, Ontario, Canada, in 1998. She is now a professor in the Department of Psychology at the University of Calgary, Calgary, Alberta, Canada. In her research, she examines several aspects of language processing in adults and in children, including word recognition processes and figurative language understanding. She is an award-winning teacher and graduate supervisor.